HOPEFUL

to

HIRED

HOW TO SCORE THE JOB YOU WANT
— STRAIGHT OUT OF COLLEGE —

ADAM S. DINCE

ISBN 13: 978-1-94-576921-4

Library of Congress Catalog Number: 2016916758
Printed in the United States of America
First Printing: 2016

20   19 18   17   16   5   4   3   2   1

Cover Design by Nupoor Gordon
Interior Design by Kim Morehead

Published by W.I. Creative Publishing, an imprint of Wise Ink Creative Publishing.

W.I. Creative Publishing
837 Glenwood Avenue
wiseinkpub.com

To order, visit seattlebookcompany.com or call (734)426-6248.
Reseller discounts available.

TABLE *of* CONTENTS

DEDICATION

"Service you pay to others is the rent
you pay for your room here on earth."

— MUHAMMAD ALI

For the last ten years of his life, my dad, Bert Dince,
made his home in Cape Cod, Massachusetts. He
was a staple in the Barnstable community and a highly respected musician. Bert taught piano to his students by day and played in many of the upper-scale
restaurants and hotels at night. He loved the Cape and
the Cape loved him back. When I would visit, we'd
hang out at his favorite jazz spots, and it was always a
sure bet that the band lead would ask my dad to sit in
for a song or two.

My dad was my hero. He was a single father. An
old yet gentle soul that was always there for those that
needed him. A humble, selfless man. Bert's spirit left
behind a legacy that I would learn much about after

he passed away.

When I arrived in the Cape to start closing out the last chapter of my dad's life, I found his teaching schedule filled with students' names and phone numbers. I knew it was my daunting responsibility to notify each of them of my father's passing. Throughout each call, I heard stories about how my dad had influenced so many lives. About how he helped his students uncover their natural musical abilities. I learned that my dad was not only a teacher to his students, but also a mentor, a father figure, and an extraordinary example of unconditional love. I know there's an old adage that says, "You can't be all things to all people." But Bert Dince was.

I learned a lot from my dad. One lesson being that taking care of people is our greatest responsibility in life. Over the years, I've tried to do my best to be just like him.

Hopeful to Hired is written in honor of my dad and dedicated to those who know where they want to go but aren't quite sure how to get there.

FOREWORD

Troy Janisch, Publisher of Social Meteor, is a digital market-ing professional and social media beatnik. He is a contributor to SmartBrief on Social Media and Social Media Today. He teaches digital marketing classes for the University of Wiscon-sin—Milwaukee and MBA classes for Saint Catherine Uni-versity in Saint Paul, MN. He leads the Social Media Analyt-ics team at U.S. Bank.

You're hopeful, and you have good reason to be: if you're a recent college grad that wants to go places, I want you to work for me. And if we have the opportunity to meet face-to-face and talk about the position, there's a good chance that I'll hire you.

Really.

The problem? You're going to be one of 250 candidates for the college-graduate-level position I have available.

You see, I work with human resources. I've told a recruiter what I'm looking for, and with that in mind, the recruiter will share the top twenty-five applicants they've picked for my position with me. You need to be in the top 10 percent of applicants, from a recruiter's point of view, for me to know anything about you. Since I'm anxious to fill my vacant position, I'll spend five to ten minutes with each resume (two to three hours between other tasks or at the end of my week) to identify six individuals that I want to talk to. You've got to make it this far—to the top 2 percent—before I have any chance to hire you.

One of the top six could be you. If not, it'll be six other candidates that might not be any better suited for the job than you are. Why am I talking to them, instead of you?

They're just better prepared.

The goal of *Hopeful to Hired* is for us to meet. That happens in one of two ways. The first method is to get you into the top 2 percent. It's about preparation. If you work in marketing or digital marketing, as Adam and I do, it means that you've got some compelling work experience, writing samples, or code examples to share. You've probably been involved in industry-related organizations, events, or communities. You might have perfect grades, but, more than that, you have an interesting life experience on your resume that makes you unforgettable.

And, of course, you've bundled all of your potential into a recruiter-friendly format that makes you a natural pick.

The second method is hacking. You've made plans to meet me outside of the hiring process. You've connected with me on LinkedIn to learn about what I do, the company I work for, and the best way for you to prepare for a career that begins on my team. You read my blog. You follow me and my company on social media. If you're also prepared (see method 1), you've done this well before I posted a job opening.

When the opening comes available, I'm already thinking of you. In fact, I've shared your name with my recruiter, so they're reaching out to you. Or, you've applied for a job on my team (or a related team), and you've sent me an e-mail to let me know so I can schedule an interview or provide a reference. You've claimed a spot in the top 2 percent, instead of only hoping for it.

Don't struggle. Don't settle.

Don't apply for a job. Apply yourself.

Be prepared and be a hacker. The jobs will come.

I hire more hackers than hopefuls.

—Troy (@socialmeteor)

INTRODUCTION

Personally Speaking

Throughout my childhood, I was more concerned about being the center of attention than I was about doing well in school. Living with unresolved issues from my parents' divorce and low self-esteem were the catalysts for a troubled adolescence.

When I finished high school, my grades were so poor that college was completely out of the question. And there I was—working a dead-end job and living at home with no way out. My grandfather, Irving Gellman, who had served in Japan during World War II, encouraged me to follow in his footsteps and join the military. So I joined the United States Navy, and the experience changed my life.

MRC (SW/AW) James Lowe was our Division Commander at Naval Recruit Basic Training and the epitome of what a drill instructor should be. When he spoke, his deep, gravelly voice put the fear of God in us. He didn't have to yell—he uttered a few words, and we knew he meant business.

For some reason Chief Lowe took a special interest in me. Maybe it was that I was out of shape and a complete mess. Maybe it was because he knew I believed in God and wanted to test my faith. Regardless, he made me his pet project. In fact, he referred to me as "Special Case Dince."

Chief Lowe was relentless. He regularly pushed me to the point where my body would give up. When I met his expectations, he'd say, "Well done, Special Case Dince!" Chief believed in me, and I welcomed his support. Eight weeks after day one of boot camp, I graduated United States Navy Basic Combat Training and reported to serve aboard an aircraft carrier, the USS *Constellation*.

On "The Connie" I found an amazing group of brothers who continued to speak those positive, encouraging words to me. Their belief in me became the fuel that fired my performance. When my active duty enlistment contract expired, I was proud to have earned an accumulation of ribbons and medals, letters of commendations, and three promotions in just three short years.

I decided not to re-enlist because I wanted to go back to school for a college education. Of course, being a horrible student throughout my childhood didn't do anything to boost my confidence that I'd succeed at the collegiate level. Fortunately for me, I found a wonderful support system of educators at Grossmont College who believed in me, mentored me, and kept me on track to graduate from both community college and San Diego State University at the top of my class. I've been so fortunate to have amazing people throughout my adult life whose mentorship and guidance helped me accomplish things I wouldn't have been able to on my own. And now, I hope to pay it forward to you—with this book.

Over the past few years, I've been able to take much of what I've learned over the course of my career and share my experiences with undergraduate students. Every year, I mentor between five and ten college students and help prepare them to be a top internship and job candidate. I'm also a regular speaker at Ad-Fed's Student Ad Summit hosted at the University of Minnesota. Plus, I am often a guest speaker at colleges and universities across the United States. Working with students is my passion. I know how hard it can be for new graduates to find a job in their field of study, and I am committed to helping in a meaningful way. I wrote this book for you, the many outstanding students I don't have the personal bandwidth to work with on a one-on-one basis. Within this book, you'll find personal stories, sound advice, and a roadmap to help guide your path to career preparation.

Professionally Speaking

When I began mentoring college students, I was surprised to learn how tough it was for many to break into their industry. See, I didn't quite follow the traditional path that most students do today. After graduation, I gave up on finding a job in my field of study and somehow fell into my career path. In fact, most people who started in digital marketing back when I did found their way into the profession by happenstance.

For example: In the early 2000s, a good friend of mine, Mitch, started an online auto-parts company. Mitch believed that he could leverage search engines to drive highly qualified traffic to his site, so, he taught himself search engine optimization (SEO) and it worked. Google became the primary source of attracting business and generated meaningful sales from people who were searching for his products. Mitch was not a marketer; he was a business owner that needed to sell his products to earn a living. A few years down the road, he sold his business and began consulting other businesses on how to do what he did. Mitch fell into online marketing.

In my case, I learned how to build websites during my junior year of college. I took this skill and turned it into a business where I built a solid roster of small business clients.

After a few years of website design, I found that I was more interested in the marketing side of the business. On a total whim, I posted my resume on a job board and was recruited for an SEO role at global digital advertising agency, iCrossing. Overnight, I went from servicing small business websites to working on top Fortune brands. My first client was Bank of America. Our results were so good that the bank increased its year-over-year budget with us from $150,000 to $4.5 million. Our success on the Bank of America account became the catalyst for my career trajectory.

A few years after accepting the role at iCrossing, I was recruited to New York City to join global digital ad agency MRM//McCann. In this role, I helped build a global search and content strategy practice along with a Center of Excellence within our Manhattan office.

From 2009 to 2012, I had the pleasure of working with globally recognized brands like ExxonMobil, Diageo, General Mills, JPMorgan Chase, and many others. In a few short years, we grew our book of business exponentially and became the most profitable (and I'll argue "successful") department in the ad agency. The combination of our team's outstanding results and fun culture elevated us to a prominent status within the agency. It also led to my promotion to Vice President of Search and Content Strategy.

In 2012, I moved to the Twin Cities to build and lead the Earned Media practice at Deluxe Corporation within the Small Business Services segment. After a few years of success at Deluxe, I moved on to an exciting new opportunity as the Director of Digital Marketing at Arrowhead Holdings. When I'm not at my day job, you'll find me teaching courses at a variety of Minnesota and Wisconsin colleges and universities.

When I started my career after college, finding a job was a much different process than it is today. The internet was in its infancy. There was no LinkedIn or any of the other popular social networks so important for finding a career today. In today's market, it is vital to create a findable professional online presence (which we'll discuss in Chapter IV). I found my first job after through an advertisement in the local paper.

Through mentoring college students, I learned about the challenges today's candidate faces. The competition is fierce, and the "old" methods of finding a job are no longer relevant. As a hiring manager, I bring the perspective of the employer to the table. I'll bring both of these points of view, that of a former candidate who used old methods and a current hiring manager watching applicants use new techniques, throughout the rest of the book.

COLLEGE WON'T TEACH YOU EVERYTHING

> "Education is the passport to the future.
> For tomorrow belongs to those who
> prepare for it today."
>
> —MALCOLM X

A Quality Education Is Just the Start

Think about this: from the very first day of kindergarten throughout your sophomore and junior years of high school, you prepared yourself to get accepted into college. And I'm guessing since you're reading this book, you've succeeded in your efforts. But just like you viewed those early years as preparatory, it's also important to view your college years as preparation for your professional life. Think of your college years as four years of opportunity to transform into an A-List job prospect upon graduation. In fact, whatever we're doing in life should be preparing us for what we want to accomplish next.

College offers a chance at a quality education that will pay off dividends the rest of our lives. One of the first classes I took in my undergraduate program was Astronomy 101. On day one, our professor, Jeff Veal, proclaimed that in order to comprehend the material, we needed to open our minds to new ways of thinking. Of course, if anyone was destined to struggle with opening the mind to new ways of thinking, it was me. I failed the first few class assignments. An overwhelming feeling of discouragement set in, and I was ready to wave the white flag of surrender.

I approached Dr. Veal with a drop card and asked him for his signature. He refused. I begged, "Dr. Veal, I'm receiving VA benefits to attend college, and I'll lose part of my funding if I fail this class. I need you to drop me." Dr. Veal told me that he wasn't going to let me fail and that he had 100 percent confidence in my abilities. So I stuck with it, Jeff kept his word, and I passed the class with an A.

I took from Dr. Veal's class far more than just an education in astronomy. I learned that it was possible for me to stretch myself, even to the point of changing the paradigms by which I thought. Prior to Dr. Veal's class, thinking outside of the box was not my norm. However, in order to understand the complex nature of physics and how they applied to astronomy, I was forced to change the way I thought. What seemed impossible to comprehend at the beginning of the course became a topic I grew passionate about. This newly discovered ability to think in new ways has allowed me to grow in both academia and in business.

I left college with a diploma in hand, a solid education in my back pocket, and all the optimism in the world that I was going to quickly land a job in my area of study. Instead, I spent months paging through the job classifieds in the local papers and applied for anything that was relevant to my passions. However, nothing seemed to stick. I remember asking myself over and over again, "Why didn't college do more to prepare me to find a good job after graduation?" I finally got hired for a job that I settled for. In hindsight, I'm grateful that things worked out the way they did. I don't know that I would have found my current career path had circumstances been any different. While I did end up falling into my current career, the first few years of job searching after graduation were lean and tough.

In the thirteen years since I finished my undergraduate program, not much has changed for college students. Most of the students I mentor or meet through guest lectures and speaking engagements face the same uncertainties that I did. Students see graduation day looming and grow afflicted with the anxiety of feeling unprepared for an internship or job search. Many of the students I mentor go to fantastic schools with excellent reputations. It's not the education that's lacking. It's the gaping void between a solid education and what it takes to find a job after graduation.

It's Not College's Job to Teach You How to Get a Job

While it would be fantastic if our schools were able to place us in a good job within our industry after college, it rarely happens. What college does provide us is the education necessary to find jobs ourselves. It doesn't hand-feed us the network, soft skills, hard skills, and online presence required in today's competitive job market.

An important lesson we learn in college is how to

operate in ambiguity, a concept we're often introduced to in casework. Other times, professors will hand out assignments intentionally lacking in the detail students would like to help ensure an accurate deliverable. While frustrating in the moment, this situation is highly useful to a student trying to prepare for the professional world: ambiguity is something that professionals face in the workplace throughout their careers, regardless of industry.

Another important lesson we learn in college is how to be resourceful. It's a place to develop skills like time management, balancing work and home life, and research techniques.

Our colleges are under no obligation to prepare us to be successful job candidates; it's up to us to use the college experience to learn resourcefulness so that we're ready for life after college. The challenge is, if we wait until the last minute to start preparing, we've already lost. And this is what nobody tells us.

Now that we've got that out of the way, the first step in preparing for post-graduate success is to pick the right major.

College Won't Pick Your Major

At some point during your college career, you'll have to decide on a major and potentially a minor. Picking a major is a "major" decision that could carry implications for the rest of your professional life. The major you choose dictates what degree you earn, which in turn is often influential in the type of career you'll be best prepared for after graduation. Nevertheless, picking a major can be challenging for a person in their late teens and early twenties. Heck, there are some of us in our forties and fifties who still haven't figured it out yet.

There will always be people born with a clear vision for their lives. A good friend of mine, Dan, knew from childhood that he wanted to be a physician. He picked Pre-Med as his undergraduate focus and then went on to medical school. He's now living his dream as a Doctor of Osteopathic Medicine.

A friend I met during my sophomore year of high school dreamed of one day becoming a director on Broadway. When he enrolled in college, he picked Theatre Arts as his major and then received his Masters of Fine Arts in Directing and Theatrical Production. After graduating, he put in years of hard work and has earned the opportunity to direct shows on

Broadway.

People with a laser focus for their lives are inspirational for sure, but we shouldn't measure ourselves against them—or anyone else for that matter. There is just as much value in using the college experience to find out what it is you'd like to pursue without necessarily knowing ahead of time. The important thing is to pace ourselves, to enjoy the college experience and pick a major when we're ready to commit.

I enrolled in college shortly after taking a job as an administrative assistant at an engineering company in San Diego. I worked directly for the Chief Financial Officer and was enjoying my exposure to the business world. In fact, business seemed a perfect fit for me. However, most members of my family were mental health professionals, and therefore I believed that psychology might be a more appropriate path than business. Deciding between the two majors became an internal conflict that caused a significant amount of anxiety.

Shortly after beginning my first semester, I met with an advisor to discuss my academic path. She provided sound advice. She recommended that I take my first year of college to immerse myself in liberal arts courses and electives. It was fun and enlightening to learn without the pressure of committing myself to a major. After finishing my freshman year, I took another look at my interests and picked business—an area I had already started gaining expertise in through my job.

So this begs the question, how do you figure out what major you should pick? If you're unsure of which major is right for you, I'll pass on the same advice that my academic advisor gave me—take your first year of college to explore a variety of options. Choose electives that stretch you and introduce you to new things. Take "Intro" classes that provide a high-level overview of the deeper subject matter. For instance, in my first year of college, I took Introduction to Psychology, Psych 101. While I thoroughly enjoyed the class, I realized that it wasn't the right profession for me.

Another method is to think "career first." Here are two questions to consider:

- Do you know what career path you want to follow?
- What job titles interest you?

A great place to start answering these questions is the LinkedIn Student App. You can find it on the iTunes App Store and Google Play. The LinkedIn Student App asks what major you've chosen and from there suggests companies and jobs you might be interested in. So plug in a few majors and see what types of job and company options LinkedIn recommends. This may help you make a more informed decision about what major to finally decide on.

Another option is to seek out professors in the majors you're considering and ask for an informational interview. During my freshman year of exploration, I took Astronomy 101 and fell in love with the subject. After the class was completed, I met with Dr. Veal to discuss the academic path of becoming an astronomer. While he encouraged me to continue down the path of astronomy, the math and physics requirements quickly voided my enthusiasm for pursuing astronomy as a major. Nevertheless, I made it a point, even after I selected business administration as my major, to continue meeting with my professors to learn more about their fields of study.

My final bit of advice about picking a major is to find a field that you love or are passionate about. Don't worry about earnings potential. Don't worry about how long of an educational commitment there is to earn the degree(s) you'll need to pursue that career path. Follow your heart. The happiest people I know are people who love what they do for a living. On average, we spend 2,080 hours a year at work. Some of us spend far more than that. Most of us will spend 30 percent of our lives working. Where do you want to spend most of your life? Crunching numbers? Teaching elementary school? Curing diseases?

Being passionate about what you do is important for the long-term success of your career and your mental well-being. It's also important to your future internship supervisors and employers that you enjoy what you do. When I hire for an entry-level role, I don't expect the new grad to have all of the skills required to be successful in the job. I just want to know that the person is the right fit for both the job and the company culture.

It costs businesses a significant amount of time and money to hire and onboard a new employee, and turnover costs businesses money as well. As such, hiring managers are always looking for people who they believe truly want to work at their company and are passionate about its mission. According to a study conducted by the Center for American Progress, employee turnover for entry-level roles costs businesses between 16–20 percent of the lost employee's salary.[1]

---

1 Heather Boushey and Sarah Jane Glynn, "There Are Significant Business Costs to Replacing Employees," Center for American Progress, November 16, 2012, https://www.americanprogress.org/wp-content/uploads/2012/11/CostofTurnover.pdf.

So if a business hires an entry-level role at $40,000 a year and the relationship doesn't work out, it will cost the business on average $7,200 to replace that position. Businesses that hire well not only reduce turnover costs, but also improve productivity and overall morale.

It's for reasons like this that Joe Hadzima, Senior Lecturer at MIT's Sloan School of Management tells businesses, ". . . be sure to devote the time to make sure that your hires are as close to perfect '10s' as possible. Anything less will be a drag on your business."[2]

While in college, try to discover something you truly love and are passionate about. It might not be your first love, but a love nevertheless. And then start working toward being proficient at it. Take it from a hiring manager, your passion will shine through in your internship and job interviews and can make all the difference between getting hired or passed over.

---

2 Joe Hadzima, "How Much Does an Employee Cost?" Boston Business Journal, http://web.mit.edu/e-club/hadzima/pdf/how-much-does-an-employee-cost.pdf.

CHAPTER I

College Won't Pick Your Friends

"Surround yourself with people who
have dreams, desire, and ambition;
they'll help you push for and realize your
own."

—UNKNOWN

In United States Naval Basic Training, I learned the importance of being surrounded with people who push us to achieve greatness. Prior to joining the military, my exercise life was non-existent. I knew that my greatest obstacle in boot camp would be passing the physical training exam.

On our third day of training, our troop embarked on our first team run. I surprised myself by completing a lap without stopping. However, as the second lap began, I found myself struggling to continue. I started to transition into give-up mode and fell behind the rest of the troop. It was then that a shipmate fell back to run alongside me. He proclaimed, "Dince, keep going, don't stop." The entire rest of the run, Booker pushed me to finish without stopping, but unfortunately, I did. However, moving forward, Booker ran alongside of me each and every run until I finished in the time required. Throughout my time in basic training, I surrounded myself with other recruits who were as dedicated to graduating as I was. And it worked.

"As iron sharpens iron, so one man sharpens another."

—PROVERBS 27:17

I could have built relationships with recruits who complained, who were negative and didn't take training seriously. There were plenty of those guys. But that would have been my demise. I never would have graduated from basic training had I chosen to build a weak foundation of friends. In fact, by the time we graduated from boot camp, we'd lost about 20 percent of the recruits we'd started with.

Think about how this applies to your collegiate career. Are you spending time with people who are focused on succeeding? Are you surrounding yourself with people who bring out the best in you? Is your collegiate network going to be there to push you when you lose motivation? If not, then it's time to get proactive about changing your network.

If you decide that it's time to freshen up your friend list, I highly recommend looking into your college's on-campus clubs and organizations and joining the ones where you're finding the right type of people. In Chapter IV, I share how joining Phi Theta Kappa, the international honor society of two-year colleges was the genesis of my current network. The group of friends that I chose to spend time with in college stills pays dividends today.

Chapter I Reflection Questions

- What are you most passionate about?
- Are there opportunities within your major to exercise those passions?
- Take a look on LinkedIn and other job sites. Are there opportunities that match your passion?
- If yes, what are they and how can you begin to prepare yourself for those roles?
- How meaningful is your circle of friends?
- What gaps have you found (if any) between what you're learning in school and what you think is applicable to finding a job post-graduation?

TAKE RISKS

"Only those who will risk going
too far can possibly find out how far
one can go."

—T.S. ELIOT

A Few Examples of Risk

Nearly every example of the success I've achieved in my life and career can be tied back to a calculated risk I've taken. Here are a couple of examples:

A JOB SWITCH:

After completing my Associate Degree in Business Administration from Grossmont College, I was offered a job on campus as a web designer. The pay was great for a college job, and the hours were flexible, which allowed me to attend university and continue working full-time. Of course, I didn't know the first thing about building web pages (which I didn't fess up to in the interview) but accepted the job offer anyway. I spent the four weeks between accepting the job offer and my start date learning as much as I could about web design. Of course, back then, web design wasn't as complex as it is today, so a small learning curve wasn't impossible. Still, it was a major risk. What if I failed? What if the four weeks I was given between accepting and starting the job wasn't enough time to learn the required foundational knowledge of web design? What if leaving the job I was happy and doing well at for this new opportunity was a bad move?

PICKING UP A NEW SKILL:

Throughout my career, one of the online marketing skill sets I wanted to learn was pay-per-click (PPC) search engine advertising. While I had serious chops in search engine optimization (SEO), PPC was a big gap in my arsenal. I knew that the only way to learn PPC was through on-the-job training. However, most of the related PPC education I received at work was either best practices or basic information. As far as learning through on-the-job training, it never happened. So I took matters into my own hands, got Google and Bing certified, and convinced a few of my freelance SEO clients to trust me with their PPC accounts. The clients who agreed to let me manage their pay-per-click advertising trusted me with thousands of dollars in monthly advertising spending. A simple misstep could have cost both the clients and me significant financial losses. Did everything turn out okay? Yes. Could it have ended much worse? It sure could have. However, I knew I was capable. And taking that leap of faith allowed me to significantly grow my freelance business.

Not All Risk Is Risk

In Chapter IV, "Get To Work," you may find yourself challenged to move out of your comfort zone to take risks or perceived risks. Essentially, risk is exposing yourself in such a way that opens you up to negative consequences. It's possible that to you, rejection is risk. Or putting yourself out there in such a way that grows your public digital footprint seems risky. Or the thought of meeting with hiring managers as an underclassman is intimidating. However, keep in mind that oftentimes, not taking the risk is actually the riskier move. Don't let fear stop you from doing what's necessary to stay ahead of the competition.

What I've found to be true in my life is that my biggest obstacle to growth is myself. My own fear of failure. My own insecurities and lack of confidence definitely play a role in the levels of anxiety I face when taking risks. However, I don't let insecurities stop me from taking risks and giving 100 percent. Neither should you.

How Do You Know Which Risks to Take?

There are risks that can lead to growth and those that can end not so positively. So how do you know which risks are appropriate to take? It's not always easy to differentiate. The key is to avoid blind risks whenever possible. To do this, I operate with a two-step decision-making model. The first step is to create a pros and cons list that scores each entry on a scale of zero to ten (ten being the highest). Once you're done writing your list, note whether the pros or cons have the highest score. Then, use the score to help you make a decision.

Find below an example of a pros and cons list I developed to help me decide whether or not to relocate from New York City to Minneapolis for a job offer:

Score	PROS	CONS	Score
10	Affordable Housing	Moving Away From Family Base	3
5	Cleaner Environment	Potential New Job Doesn't Work Out	10
7	Less Crowded	Moving From A Tier 1 To Tier 3 Market	10
10	Competitive Salary	No Friend Base	5
10	No More Subway	Moving Away From Solid Business Network	8
8	Dog Will Have More Room	Leaving A Place Where I Have A Great Reputation	10
3	Expand Network	Long Winters	3
7	New Experience In eCommerce	Remote Boss	3
8	Get Experience In-House vs. Agency	Fewer Big Named Concerts	1
2	Explore New Parts of The Country	What If I Don't Enjoy Living In Minnesota?	8
5	Great Agency Life		
5	Big Corporate Base		
7	Further Away From Family Drama		
87			61

As you can see in the table above, the pros outweighed the cons. This is one of the two methods I use in assessing whether or not to take a risk.

The other method I use is listening to my intuition. I've heard others refer to this as "Listening to your gut," "Listening to the Holy Spirit," and other variations. Regardless of what you call it, you should feel peace about a risk you're evaluating. Keep in mind: fear and peace can go together. You can be scared about something, yet still have peace about it. When I made the decision to move to Minneapolis from New York City, was I scared? Heck yes! Did I have insecurities about whether or not it was the right call? Of course. However, there was a peace I had inside reaffirming that my choice was the right move.

A year after I relocated to Minneapolis, a local digital marketing agency began courting me to join their company in a leadership role. I was friendly with most of the staff, and it seemed like a no-brainer. I could once again work on a portfolio of all-star brands. I could work in a super-cool office space that inspired creativity. There were so many positives. After completing my pros and cons list, my pro score outweighed the cons. However, I missed the peace that I grew accustomed to feeling when making good risk decisions. My intuition told me not to pursue the opportunity—so I politely declined.

A year later, the ad agency lost a lot of its talent, and I learned things about its operations that would have made it an unpleasant work experience. At the end of the day, not taking the job was the right call. Throughout most of my life, listening to my intuition has paid off, and I never go against it. Keep in mind, intuition takes time to develop, and for some it comes more naturally than for others. This is one reason why creating a "pros and cons" list is so important; it allows you to chart out what you perceive to be positive and negative aspects of a situation while incorporating your professional instincts that may not have fully developed.

Developing Intuition

My best advice to those who are deciding whether or not to take a specific risk is to listen to their intuition. This can be tricky: some people question the authenticity of their intuition and ask how to further develop it. I oftentimes find this with college students I mentor.

A few months ago, I caught up with Maria, an outside sales professional that I'd mentored while she was in college. Maria was finishing her first year of a job that she accepted right out of college and was in the process of interviewing for a new opportunity. Her pros and cons list was pretty even on both sides, but Maria was enticed by the thought of taking a new job that would allow her to move cross-country and fast-track into management. We spoke ad nauseam about her pros and cons list but kept finding ourselves talking in circles. So I asked Maria if she had peace about taking the new role and what her intuition was telling her. She shared that the new opportunity scared her and that she also lacked the peace about taking the role. Maria opted not to take the job and in hindsight, is happy she declined.

Think about getting married. You meet the person of your dreams, date for a few years, and get engaged. As the wedding date gets closer, one or both of you start to get cold feet. The fear of committing yourself to the same person for the rest of your life starts to creep in. The fear might even be crippling. However, in your heart, you know this is the right person for you—so you overcome your fear and live life happily ever after.

On the flip side: You meet the person of your dreams, date for a few years, and get engaged. But throughout the relationship you have doubts that this is the right person for you. As the wedding date approaches, you find yourself not necessarily scared but without peace about getting married. In your heart, you know it's the wrong decision, and you make the decision to end the engagement before it's too late.

Developing intuition is a lifelong process. Once you get the hang of it and start exercising your intuitive muscles, the stronger it will get. The key to developing your intuition is learning to spot it and then trust it. Here are three tips to get you started:

1. **Spend time with yourself:** You'll read plenty of articles and books that instruct you to find a quiet spot, sit, and meditate. For me, this approach doesn't work well. What does work for me is running. When I run, my mind clears

which allows me to become more in tune with my subconscious. In fact, the idea to write this book came to me while I was running.

When I lived in New York City, I took the subway everywhere. On subway rides, I'd put my on headphones, get in "the zone," and use the commutes to think about things going on in my life. Whether there were important decisions weighing on mind, potential business opportunities to consider, or topics to think about for my next article, so many points of clarity occurred during these commutes. Again, I was not in a quiet room with a meditation tape playing. I was listening to music on a crowded subway, with little room to myself. I share this because it's important for you to know that the methods that work for others may not work for you. The only way you'll learn what jives best with your style is to try different things and see what sticks.

2. **Free-Flow Writing:** Free-flow question writing can help you tap into what's really causing you uncertainty about a decision. For example, say you're debating about which major to pick.

You've identified a few options but can't quite make a decision about which to go with. Take out a notepad and start writing as many questions about the decision as possible. Don't think about the questions you're writing—just write. When you're finished writing, review your questions and try to identify common themes. Are you unsure about the career trajectory that the majors provide? Are you equally interested in each of the majors? Is there a major you really want to pick but are intimidated by the workload and time commitment? Free-flow writing will help you get in touch with what's going on in your mind. Being in touch with your subconscious is vital to listening to your intuition.

3. **Journal:** In the previous step, we spoke about tapping into your subconscious through free-flow question writing. Journaling is a bit different. It focuses on keeping a written account of your thoughts, feelings, experiences, etc. Journaling is a practice common among successful people. For example: let's say your professor assigns you to a group where you have grave concerns about the quality of work or level of effort

your classmates might put forth. Maybe you don't know the other students well, but your gut tells you that something's off. The opposite may also happen. You might find yourself assigned to a group you're thrilled to be a part of. Either way, keep a journal and note your observations. Pay close attention to what you're feeling and sensing when you go through these situations, write down your thoughts on the matter, and then afterwards, ask questions like:

- Was your intuition right or wrong?
- Are you getting better at clearly hearing your intuition?

I highly recommend working through some of these exercises as soon as possible. Start right now. Your ability to listen to your intuition and take calculated risks can help you both in school and after graduation. The sooner you're able to effectively listen to your gut, the better off you'll be in your personal life and career.

Chapter II Reflection Questions

- What are some risks you've taken in your life?
- If you've taken risks, how did they turn out?
- If you've taken risks, in hindsight, is there anything you'd do differently?
- Think of three times your intuition has been accurate.
- Have there been times you believe your intuition was off?
- Have you ever ignored your intuition? If so, what was the outcome?
- What are some practices or habits you can use to strengthen your ability to listen to your intuition?
- What risks stand in front of you now that you can use your intuition as a guide?

CHAPTER III

THE SOFT SKILLS MATTER

"Soft skills get little respect, but will make or break your career."

—PEGGY KLAUS

Why Soft Skills Are Important

If you search the web, you'll find a variety of definitions of the term "soft skills" from a plethora of trusted sources. As it applies to one's career, I lean toward Lei Han, Stanford Engineer and Wharton MBA's definition. "These are the skills we use to interact with others at work. Examples of people skills include communications and interpersonal skills as well as skills to manage upwards and deal with office politics." [3]

According to the Multi-Generational Job Search Study in 2014, conducted by Millennial Branding, "Based on the data, acquiring a college degree is important, but may take a backseat to an applicant's personality. In fact, 73 percent of hiring managers felt that colleges are only 'somewhat preparing' students for the working world. The biggest challenges facing hiring managers seem to be how the job seeker presents themselves—36 percent of HR Pros reported that candidates are 'unprepared' and 33 percent said they have a 'bad attitude' when interviewing." [4]

In a different study conducted by CareerBuilder, Rosemary Haefner, Vice President of Human Resources says:

> When companies are assessing job candidates, they're looking for the best of both worlds: someone who is not only proficient in a particular function, but also has the right

3 Lei Han, "Soft Skills Definition: What Are Soft Skills?" Soft Skills—Ask a Wharton MBA, https://bemycareercoach.com/softskills/what-are-soft-skills.

4 Dan Schawbel, "The Multi-Generational Job Search Study 2014," Millennial Branding, May 20, 2014, http://millennialbranding.com/2014/multi-generational-job-search-study-2014/.

personality . . . Along with responsibilities, it's important to highlight soft skills that can give employers an idea of how quickly you can adapt and solve problems, whether you can be relied on to follow through and how effectively you can lead and motivate others.[5]

Additionally, the CareerBuilder study goes on to read:

The vast majority of employers—77 percent—believe that soft skills (less tangible skills associated with one's personality, such as a positive attitude) are just as important as hard skills (skills that are learned to perform a specific job function and can be measured, such as operating a computer program). Sixteen percent of employers said soft skills are more important than hard skills when evaluating candidates for a job.[6]

So, how do you develop your soft skills?

---

[5] "Overwhelming Majority of Companies Say Soft Skills Are Just as Important as Hard Skills, According to a New CareerBuilder Survey," CareerBuilder, April 10, 2014.

[6] "Overwhelming Majority of Companies," CareerBuilder.

Practice Your Soft Skills

There's an old saying that goes, "You never get a second chance to make a good first impression." It's true for the most part, and matured soft skills will help you make that good first impression.

When you start applying for internships and jobs, you'll find that if a company calls you in for an interview, they're already comfortable with what's on your resume and with what they've learned about you from the information available online. The in-person meeting is certainly to learn more about you and your experience, but even more so, it's about chemistry: an interviewer is trying to gauge whether or not you're a good fit for the company and the team you'll be working with. Your goal coming out of a first, second, and third job interview is to let your personality shine through, to connect with potential colleagues and leadership, and to assess how well you jive with the organization's culture.

Developing your soft skills while in college will help you build relationships with mentors, grow networks, and successfully navigate the internship and full-time job processes. Many of you already have strong soft skills but haven't practiced using them in the right environments. For instance, with your friends you might be the center of attention. However, when put into a professional setting, your nerves get the best of you.

What I want you to take from this section is that soft skills are really just people skills. The better you are with people, the better your career prospects will be. This holds true for post-collegiate employment as well as for the rest of your professional career. The idea is to get better at interacting with people in a personal way in a variety of settings. College offers you the opportunities to put yourselves into professional settings to exercise those soft skills.

CLUBS AND ORGANIZATIONS

On-campus clubs and organizations not only provide you with a fantastic opportunity to network, but also to grow your soft skills in a professional environment. During my freshman and sophomore years of college, I served in a variety of leadership roles within Phi Theta Kappa, the international honor society of two-year colleges.

As President of the Grossmont College Chapter of Phi Theta Kappa, I regularly met with the college president, Dr. Ted Martinez. The more I met with Dr. Martinez on a one-on-one basis, the more comfortable I grew being myself in a professional setting.

Look for on-campus clubs and organizations that will allow you the opportunity to spend time with staff in formal surroundings.

OFFICE HOURS

In my junior year at San Diego State University, I ended up in a rigorous class with an extremely tough professor. If one of us asked a question and didn't use proper business terminology, he'd insist that we re-phrase the question appropriately before he'd answer. He was such a personality that he told us his first name was not Victor, it was "Professor." One afternoon, I visited Victor during office hours to chat about course material I was struggling with. I recall the anxiety of waiting for Victor to turn away from his computer and address me.

Looking around Victor's office, I noticed a family photo on his desk. It humanized him and put me more at ease. I complimented Victor on his beautiful family and he thanked me. He spoke briefly about his wife and children. This led to a personal conversation that allowed us to get better acquainted. Future classes were much more enjoyable.

After this experience, I made it a point to schedule time with my professors during office hours. Doing so helped me get a better feel for different personality types that I would come to encounter post-graduation. In hindsight, office hours helped me navigate the personal side of the interview process and post-hire relationships with leadership.

Consider meeting with your professors during office hours. Practice presenting yourself in a professional way while letting your personality shine through. When meeting with professors during office hours:

- Let them know that you would like to be critiqued on your soft skills post meeting. Constructive criticism should be welcomed.
- Ask professors to conduct mock internship and job interviews. Most likely, they were either managers or hiring managers at some point in their careers.
- Once you've completed their course, add professors on LinkedIn and keep in touch.

Keep in mind that these types of requests should only come after developing a relationship with your professors. You can't do these things after the first week of class. There are proactive things you can do to start building a professional connection with you professors:

- Ask good questions in class

- Be a part of class discussions
- E-mail your professors follow-up questions after class
- When you arrive to class, properly greet your professors

Remember, we're talking about soft skills/people skills. The key here is to hone your people skills. Also, know that building relationships with your professors will help prepare you for building relationships with leadership at your first job out of college.

GROUP PROJECTS

Alas, the dreaded group projects. Group projects are academic cornerstones in both undergraduate and graduate programs. Granted, in group projects you're not necessarily communicating with professors or staff—however, you're forced to interact with your classmates in a professional manner. Leveraging your soft skills with friends and classmates is easy because there's no agenda. The same could be said about colleagues attending a happy hour after work. However, it's important to exercise your soft skills when thrust in to a working environment where non-formal pleasantries go away. After working in a group, ask the members for feedback on your soft skills. Constrictive criticism is critical for growth.

Understanding Emotional Intelligence (EI)

"If your emotional abilities aren't in hand, if you don't have self-awareness, if you are not able to manage your distressing emotions, if you can't have empathy and have effective relationships, then no matter how smart you are, you are not going to get very far."

—Daniel Goleman

Among academics, there is debate about whether emotional intelligence is defined as a soft skill or something entirely different. For the purposes of this chapter, let's classify it as a soft skill. *Psychology Today* defines emotional intelligence (EI) as "the ability to identify and manage your own emotions and the emotions of others."[7]

Daniel Goleman, who in many people's opinions is the subject matter authority on emotional intelligence, argues, " . . . it was not cognitive intelligence that guaranteed business success but emotional intelligence." [8]

As you begin to follow the advice in Chapter IV, "Get To Work," you'll find that a portion of the strategy involves developing relationships with a variety of professionals in your future industry while you're still in college. While emotional intelligence takes time to develop and improves with age, you should be aware of its common components and understand how each might factor into landing your first job out of school.

In his *Harvard Business Review* article, "What Makes a Leader," Daniel Goleman introduces us to the five components of emotional intelligence: *Self-awareness*, *self-regulation*, motivation, empathy, and social skill.[9] Here's how the components apply to you, right now, where you are in your education and

---

7 "What Is Emotional Intelligence?" Psychology Today, https://www.psychologytoday.com/basics/emotional-intelligence.

8 Chris Golis, "A Brief History of Emotional Intelligence," Practical Emotional Intelligence, http://www.emotionalintelligencecourse.com/eq-history.

9 Daniel Goleman, "What Makes a Leader?" *Harvard Business Review*, January, 2004, https://hbr.org/2004/01/what-makes-a-leader.

professional career:

Self-Awareness: Relates to your knowing your strengths, weaknesses, drives, values, and impact on others. Essentially, self-awareness is all about knowing whom you are as a person and being able to use this understanding to present yourself effectively.

- **Recognize your *strengths*:** This allows you to continue to develop in those areas and use them as differentiators as you begin to network and build your personal tribes.

- **Recognize your *weaknesses*:** At the very least, recognizing your weaknesses allows you to be aware of certain areas that challenge you. For example, I'm aware that one of my weaknesses occurs in conversations or group discussions. While others are talking, I find myself thinking of what to say next. This keeps me from giving my full attention to those speaking and can hinder my ability to contribute. Being self-aware allows me to recognize when I'm not actively listening so I can course correct. There are thought-leaders in the emotional intelligence community who believe that our weaknesses are difficult to change and that we should focus on our strengths instead of attempting to improve our weaknesses. I agree that there is some truth to that. However, I'm also a believer in learning how to become the best version of yourself and trying to shore up the weaknesses you can.

Being self-aware of your weaknesses is an integral part of being able to develop them into strengths. However, also know, even the most self-aware people aren't aware of everything. It's okay to ask others what they think our weaknesses are. And it is okay to accept constructive criticism from others.

- **Recognize what *drives* you:** This allows you to make better informed decisions about which job opportunities to take and which to politely pass by. As it applies to me, I know that I'm results-driven. In order to feel rewarded in a career, I need to see results. For instance, my primary concern with this book is not so much how many people buy it, but rather how many people it helps. If someone offered me a lump sum of cash to write a book that simply collects dust on shelves, I wouldn't write it. I've learned this about myself through trial and error. I've taken some consulting jobs just for the money, and while they're sometimes a necessary evil, I find it challenging to stay focused on those types of gigs.

- **Understand your *values*:** Keep in mind that when networking and looking for a job, you're going to feel most connected to people who share similar values to you. And this applies vice versa. For example: values like honor, commitment, and courage are important to me and drive my personal and professional philosophies. And it's important that my friends, business partners, employers, and the people that I hire share similar values.

  If someone were to ask you today what your values are—what would you say? And how would you define them? In my case, honor, courage, and commitment were solidified for me during my time serving in the military. In fact, they are the core values of the United States Navy.

What do they mean, and how do they apply to me? Personally and professionally:

- **Honor:** We respect each other regardless of rank or position. It also means that we keep our word and behave both ethically and morally.
- **Courage:** To make the right decision, even if it goes against popular opinion. It's our dedication to doing the right thing, even if there are negative consequences for doing so.
- **Commitment:** Being committed to each other as a team, family, and country. To be committed to the goals and missions of the organizations we work for. To be committed to upholding both honor and courage.

- **Understand your *impact on others*:** It's important to know how your words and actions affect others, both positively and negatively. Have you ever had someone tell you that your smile made their day? Or that your words encourage them? Maybe you've had a bad day and acted in a way that hurt someone's feelings. It's important to be aware of how you impact others. The more aware you are, the more successful you'll be at improving your interactions and relationships with others.

Self-Regulation: Relates to controlling or redirecting destructive impulses and moods. Have you ever been in a bad mood and let those negative feelings control your responses to situations you're in? Have you ever been in a situation where someone says something that pulled on an emotional trigger which caused you to respond without first taking a deep breath or a timeout? We all have—and most of us still do. The key is to work on improving our self-regulation skills, and college is a great place to practice.

I had the distinct honor of working for a top-notch CEO at my first professional job after the Navy. One of his values was loyalty—and we were all aware of how much it bothered him when an employee left the company. I recall an afternoon when a senior engineer quit the company without giving the CEO a proper two-week notice. I expected to hear shouting and a few coarse words float out of the CEO's office but didn't hear a peep.

Later that afternoon, the CEO stopped by my desk and poured himself and me a glass of Crown and Coke. Word of the resignation had circulated throughout the company by then, and everyone wanted to know the gory details about what had gone down. I asked the CEO if he had countered the engineer's offer to keep him at the company, to which he replied that he didn't counter offers as a policy. He said, "If an employee doesn't want to be here, he should go." I then asked the CEO what he said to the engineer after he resigned. The CEO replied that he had been upset but through self-regulation avoided saying anything too brash; he said that he would sleep on it and address it the next day.

After our conversation, I kept thinking about what I would have said to the engineer had I been the CEO. I probably would have reacted immediately and said things I'd regret later. I was impressed with the CEO's ability to self-regulate—especially since it was a weakness of mine at the time. Nearly twenty years later, I think about that day all the time. It's a constant reminder to me to regulate my responses. Am I perfect at it? No. No one is. However, it's important that we always work on getting better at self-regulation.

Good self-regulation skills can help you build and maintain meaningful relationships with others. In the business world, relationships are everything and are so vital to landing that good first job after college.

You'll find that mentors or people in your network are more willing to recommend you and even hire you if they like you and trust that you're even keel. Sure, we all have our moments when we aren't able to control our reactions to certain stimuli. Maybe someone tells a joke that offends us, or we're asked to do something we don't want to do. In the professional world, there are many instances where some stimulus can get the best of us. However, the more we are aware of our behavior, the better we will be at controlling our reactions to external stimuli. And the better we're able to regulate our emotions, the more successful we'll be in our professional lives. Especially as you build your networks and relationships, which you'll read more about in Chapter IV.

Motivation: Relates to how motivated you get by achieving goals. The higher level of motivation you have, the more successful you'll be landing that first job out of school. People with high motivation remain positive even when they feel the deck is stacked against them.

People with strong motivation enjoy being stretched. We constantly optimize to improve results, learn from our mistakes, and push to achieve beyond expectation. Our desire to achieve is not for the accolades that come from our success. It's being driven by our intrinsic need to achieve.

On the flip side, not everyone has an intense level of motivation. However, the good news is that there are ways to maximize your motivation. For example:

Eliminate Distractions: I cannot underscore this point enough. With all of the stimuli around us (e.g., our phones, tablets, other commitments), it's so easy to get distracted. One thing I've learned about myself is that when I have too many other things going on in life outside of work, the less motivated and productive I am at the office.

A few years ago, I joined the boards of a couple of organizations. What I didn't realize was how much time, energy, and commitment those board roles required. When I found that the commitments I had made to these organizations caused me to lose motivation at work, I knew something needed to change. So I resigned one of my board memberships. I also learned through this experience not to overcommit myself to things. Being overcommitted to too many things can absolutely hinder motivation.

Set Goals That Motivate You: Maybe getting a job after graduating from college is not a goal that motivates you right now. If so, that's completely understandable. College takes so much of the present moment that it's difficult to get motivated about preparing for life after college. In this case, think of other goals that would motivate you to start preparing to land that job after college without that being your sole focus. For instance, maybe your goal is to pay down your student loans in a certain period of time after graduation. Maybe your goal is to not live at home with your parents after graduation. Either way, if you're not finding yourself motivated, look to set goals that pull on triggers that do motivate you.

Empathy: is the ability to connect with other people's feelings and emotions. You may soon find yourself in an interview for an internship. As you're pitching your abilities to the interviewer, you notice that he or she is silent or not saying much. While this might deter a person with a lower level of empathy, it doesn't discourage you. Why? Because though the interviewer isn't saying much, you notice that her body language shows interest in what you're saying. So you keep going and nail the interview because you were able to understand and play off the body language cues that the interviewer gave.

You may also find yourself leading an on-campus student organization. As the team's leader, you must be able to sense and understand the viewpoints of everyone on the board and various committees. People with empathy can read body language and other nonverbal communication cues. People with empathy thoughtfully consider people's feelings along with other elements when making informed decisions. Being able to understand and relate to others will help you navigate the "people" aspect of being a top job prospect, not to mention helping in every other aspect of your life where relationships are involved.

Social Skill: is the culmination of all of the above components of emotional intelligence. Social skill is what allows you to build successful networks of people. It allows you to influence others. To get people behind your vision. Social skill is the key to emotional intelligence.

It is believed that everyone is born with some level of EI and then over the course of our lives we naturally develop it. Think about it as nature vs. nurture. Nature determines how much emotional intelligence we're born with, and nurture is what helps us grow it. I've given you some ideas about ways you can improve each of the elements of your EI. However, also know that EI is part of who you are. It's part of your personality. It takes time to evolve. Again, nurture plays an important role in our maturation of emotional intelligence. Throughout your life, as you're faced with new opportunities, challenges, and stimuli, your EI will grow.

If this concept of emotional intelligence interests you, and you'd like to learn more about your level of EI, I recommend the University of California, Berkeley online assessment tool.[10]

Additionally, most traditional colleges and universities offer psychology, sociology, and business courses that dive deep into the topic of EI. Earlier we spoke about the fact that college won't teach you everything. However, college does offer many opportunities to learn about yourself. I highly recommend, if you're not already in one of the above-mentioned majors, taking an elective that covers EI. The time and investment will be well spent.

---

10 "Body Language Quiz: Test Your Emotional Intelligence," Greater Good: The Science of a Meaningful Life, http://greatergood.berkeley.edu/ei_quiz/.

In the next section, we'll cover a few of the available tools that you can use to learn more about your personality type and strengths, which all play a part in the development of your soft skills.

Tools of the Trade

As you develop your soft skills, there are two tools or assessments that I recommend. The first is the Myers-Briggs Type Indicator personality assessment.

The second is the Clifton StrengthsFinder assessment. Both of these resources will help you learn more about yourself.

MYERS-BRIGGS TYPE INDICATOR (MBTI)

I was formally introduced to the Myers-Briggs Type Indicator (MBTI) during my first year of MBA studies at St. Catherine University. The MBTI is a questionnaire that asks a variety of questions about personality and preferences. After all questions are answered, the MBTI takes your input and places you in one of sixteen personality types. The purpose of the MBTI is to help us understand how we perceive the world and make decisions.

Knowing your MBTI personality type will not only

help you better understand yourself, but will also allow you to better communicate the value of your personality type in interviews, whether they be informational in nature or for internships and permanent jobs.

According to the Myers-Briggs Type Indicator assessment, my personality type is ENTP. ENTP stands for Extraversion, Intuition, Thinking, and Perceiving. We ENTPs view limitations as challenges to be overcome, provide new ways to do things, take initiative, spur others on, and encourage independence in others. We are also very change oriented. This is a highly accurate description of who I am, both personally and professionally.

(ENTP WordCloud)[11]

Typically in job interviews, one of the first things you will be asked to do is tell the interviewer about yourself. Personalizing your MBTI results and putting together an elevator pitch about your personality type can help you impress the interviewer. Here's an example of how I might use my MBTI results to answer a question:

"At my very core, I'm an extravert. I get energy from being around other people. My extraversion is a key part of what allows me

---

11 Neojungian Academy, http://erikthor.com/.

to build and manage thriving teams. Additionally, I really do believe that everyone has unique talents and gifts that make them who they are. When I manage practices and teams, I encourage others to be the best versions of themselves. This goes a long way in terms of building equity with coworkers, colleagues, and employees. I'm also the type of person who always looks for new and better ways of doing things. I believe there are always opportunities to improve. Finally, I enjoy being challenged. In fact, I need a constant stretch in my goals. It keeps me motivated."

I am a huge fan of hiring new college graduates. In fact, in my past few roles, all but one hire have been new grads. Since most new college graduates haven't had the opportunity to build a wealth of professional experience, I dig deep to learn as much about them as I can. It's important for me to understand how a candidate thinks and how well they are able to respond to vague inquiries like, "Tell me about yourself." As you begin to build professional networks (which we discuss in Chapter IV) and engage in job interviews, I guarantee you'll be asked to share a bit about yourself. Use your MBTI results to help you get that elevator pitch ready.

I highly recommend taking the MBTI instrument and learning about your personality type. I recommend the MBTI online resource.[12]

THE CLIFTON STRENGTHSFINDER ASSESSMENT

The previous section introduced you to the MBTI and how it helps you get a better understanding of your personality and preferences. The other soft skills tool I recommend is the Gallup Organization's Clifton StrengthsFinder assessment.[13]

The Clifton StrengthsFinder poses a variety of scenarios to you, which you respond to on a measured scale.

---

12 MBTI, last modified 2016, https://www.mbtionline.com/.

13 Tom Rath, Strengthsfinder 2.0 (New York: Gallup Press, 2007).

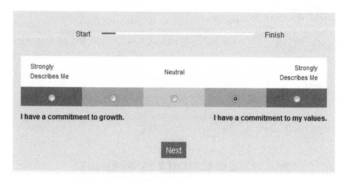

After you complete the assessment, you'll receive a list of your strengths accompanied by detailed explanations of each. As the name implies, the Clifton StrengthsFinder assessment helps us better understand our strengths and encourages us to play to those strengths as opposed to dwelling on our weaknesses (or strengths we don't have). Knowing what your strengths are is vital to pitching yourself as an A-list job prospect.

The StrengthsFinder is used in many organizations today. For example: David Reimer, former Vice President of Marketing at Yahoo, needed to pick the right employee to fill a crucial role. As he browsed through his team's StrengthsFinder results, he came across a member who scored very well on a particular strength that was needed for the job. So Reimer decided to give her a shot and she delivered.[14]

(StrengthsFinder2.0 assessment included with purchase)

My core strength categories, as illustrated in my StrengthsFinder2.0 results, are *influencing* and *relationship building*. "People who are innately good at influencing are always selling the team's ideas inside and outside the organization. When you need someone to take charge, speak up, and make sure your

---

14 Susan Adams, "The Test That Measures A Leader's Strength," Forbes, August 28, 2009, http://www.forbes.com/2009/08/28/strengthsfinder-skills-test-leadership-managing-jobs.html.

group is heard, look to someone with the strength to influence. Relationship builders are the glue that holds a team together. Strengths associated with bringing people together—whether it is by keeping distractions at bay or keeping the collective energy high—transform a group of individuals into a team capable of carrying out complex projects and goals."[15] You should take the StrengthsFinder 2.0 assessment as a college student. Knowing your strengths as you start networking and interviewing for internships and jobs will take you a long way.

Typically in an interview, whether it is informational in nature or an actual job interview, you'll be asked to describe your strengths. You must be prepared to respond to the best of your ability. The StrengthsFinder assessment can help you not only identify your strengths, but provide you the information to be able to explain them in context to the interviewer.

Much of what we've covered in *Hopeful to Hired* thus far pertains to gaining a better understanding of who you are as a person and direction on how to develop the soft skills needed to launch your career while still in college.

15 "StrengthsFinder Leadership Themes," Strengths Test, http://www. strengthstest.com/strengthsfinder-leadership-themes.

Chapter III Reflection Questions

- What are your strongest soft skills?
- What soft skills do you need to improve upon?
- How have your soft skills helped you?
- Have your soft skills ever failed you?
- How would you rate your emotional intelligence (EI)?
- Do you know anyone who has found a career doing what they love to do?
- If so, have you reached out for an informational interview?
- What do you think your strengths are?
- What about your personality could you showcase in a job interview?

GET TO WORK

Introduction

Now that we've spent some time focusing on the philosophical aspects of finding success after your undergraduate program, let's get to work on implementing strategies that you can use to land a job in your field.

As I mentioned earlier in the book, I mentor between five and ten undergraduate students every year. I've been blessed to see each and every one of them thrive post-graduation. Throughout the course of my mentorship, I've learned so much about what it takes for college students to stand out from the competition. The recommendations provided in this chapter are the culmination of what I know will work.

Keep in mind, you may be reading this book a few years after publication. While some of the advice will speak to specific social networks and relevant technology, the underlying theory is what matters. As technology continues to advance, know that you'll be able to apply the book's pedagogy to whatever the latest and greatest innovations are. Some points to keep in mind this chapter:

1. Not all recommendations may be appropriate for you.
2. Do not avoid a recommendation because it makes you uncomfortable. Keep in mind that being uncomfortable with a recommendation does not mean that it is not appropriate for you.
3. While I can't guarantee that these recommendations will land you the job of your dreams, they will definitely give you in the best possible opportunity to do so.
4. Have fun with the content.
5. This is sound advice for landing your first job after college and is also applicable for future career endeavors.

Additionally, at the time I wrote *Hopeful to Hired*, Microsoft announced its acquisition of LinkedIn. Within this chapter, you'll find strategic LinkedIn recommendations based on how LinkedIn is built and organized today. In the coming months or years, Microsoft may change the way LinkedIn operates, but much of the philosophy I share should apply to LinkedIn, regardless of future iterations.

Networking With A Purpose

"The richest people in the world look for
and build networks; everyone else looks
for work."

—ROBERT KIYOSAKI

Talk to anyone who's successful in life and they'll attribute much of their accomplishments to their ability to network with a purpose. It's not enough to network—you must thoughtfully network. Before reading further into specific networking strategies, answer the three questions below to help make this endeavor as successful as possible.

1. What do you want to accomplish through networking?
2. What types of people do you need to meet in order to make networking meaningful to your career?

3. Where do those people network?

Know that everyone you meet has the opportunity to positively influence your life—and vice versa. Think of the friends you have in your life at this moment. You probably met a few of them through some sort of networking activity. Over time, you built strong friendships. And I'm sure those friends have done meaningful things for you and you for them. Keep this in mind as you read through the next sections. While it's important to network with a purpose, you also don't want to miss out on a great connection because they don't necessarily meet your initial search criteria.

Networks to Find The Right Mentor

We all need mentors. A good mentor will inspire you to reach higher and dig deeper and can often see potential in you that you may not see in yourself. If you're putting forth the effort and earn the mentor's respect, they can help open doors for you that you might not have noticed otherwise.

I ended the first semester of my freshman year of college with a perfect 4.0 GPA. Don't get me wrong, I took mostly easy classes. Shortly after receiving my grades, I was invited to join the international honor society of two-year colleges, Phi Theta Kappa. I regularly attended chapter meetings, volunteered for fundraisers, and made it a point to befriend the chapter's faculty, staff, and student leadership.

After one of our monthly meetings, the chapter president approached me with an idea. "Adam, my term is coming to an end. Our current vice president, Nathan, is going to run for chapter president, and I think you should run for the VP role."

I replied, "No way, Darren. I am so not qualified to hold any sort of leadership role in an honor society." As I mentioned earlier in the book, I was a horrible high school student and even though I did well in my first semester of college, I didn't believe my results were sustainable. Furthermore, my high school failures made me feel like an imposter at the collegiate level—especially as a member of an honor society.

Nevertheless, Darren responded, "Adam, you are qualified and you'll do a damn good job." So I took the leap, ran for office, and bested three other people for the role. Shortly after assuming the role of vice president, our new chapter president, Nathan, resigned. Nine months after starting my college career, I became the president of Grossmont College's Phi Theta Kappa.

As my term as chapter president came to a close,

my faculty advisor and mentor, Israel Cardona, asked if I'd be interested in running for a leadership role at the regional level. I asked what the job would entail. He explained that the region was comprised of over sixty Phi Theta Kappa chapters across Nevada and California and that the regional board was charged with oversight and conference planning. While the level of responsibility of this role intimidated me, I decided to go for it. I trusted that if I were elected, Israel's guidance and mentorship would fill any of the gaps I had in preparation for the job. A few months later, I assumed the role of the president of the Nevada/California region of Phi Theta Kappa.

My two years serving as a Phi Theta Kappa officer allowed me to develop strong relationships with our college president, Dr. Ted Martinez, and his staff. Dr. Martinez was a fantastic mentor and someone who took great interest in my life. While Dr. Martinez had a full plate as the leader of Grossmont College, he always made time for me. As you're well aware of, college life can make the best of us feel a bit insecure. Many of us travel away from home or live off campus. Unlike high school, college offers far less hand-holding and is very much a transitional phase in our lives. Dr. Martinez helped me navigate through this time with genuine care and leadership. He too was able to see abilities in me that I didn't see in myself.

Shortly before I graduated with my Associates Degree, Dr. Martinez invited me to his office for a quick meeting. When I arrived, Dr. Martinez shared how much Grossmont College appreciated my leadership in Phi Theta Kappa and as a student. He knew that once I transferred to San Diego State University, I would not be able to keep working a fulltime eight to five job and maintain a high GPA. Dr. Martinez asked me to stay on at Grossmont College as an employee. He offered me a new role he created as an on-campus web designer. This job would allow me to attend university full time and continue to earn enough money to live comfortably while pursuing my undergraduate degree. It was a no-brainer. I gladly accepted.

I owe much of where I am today to that role as a web developer at Grossmont College. In fact, I wouldn't be where I am today without the support system and community who believed in me enough to push me further than I would have made it on my own.

I have had so many wonderful mentors, whom I owe the most incredible amount of gratitude toward. And I met all of these people by taking advantage of networking opportunities. As you network and meet potential mentors, formally ask them to take on a mentoring role. Often, mentors are willing to take you under their wings but don't necessarily want to be presumptuous and offer.

How do you know whom to ask to be a mentor? Here are three things I consider:

- Does the person take a genuine interest in my life?
- Is the person successful in both professional and personal life?
- Is this the type of person whose footsteps I'd like to follow in?

Earlier in the book, we spoke about intuition. As you build out your networks, which we talk about in the following sections, use the intuition you have and are developing to find the right mentors.

Use Informational Interviews to Build Your Network

Informational interviews are both a great way to learn more about the type of jobs and careers you're interested in as well as opportunities to find mentors. Also look at professionals who make themselves available for informational interviews as opportunities to grow your network. Every year, I typically give a half dozen or so informational interviews to students who ask. Many of the students or interns whom I've met with are still part of my network. I find that through informational interviews and mentoring, I get as much back—if not more—as I give. And my rule is if a student inspires me, I invest my time, energy, and resources into them.

A student I met with a few years ago shared, among other things, that she would be the first member of her family to graduate from college. As she spoke about her family life, I saw many similarities to mine. Her story resonated with me because, like her, I too had to overcome the odds. It became my mission to make sure that she was taken care of post-graduation. We worked together throughout the remainder of her senior year, focusing on many of the things you're reading about in this book. Fortunately for me, a role opened up on my team that she was a perfect for, so we hired her. Since then, we've both left Deluxe, but she continues to flourish in her career.

More than anything else, an informational interview is your chance to turn a one-time meeting into a lifelong connection. To start, find someone who is either doing what you want to do career-wise or is the hiring manager within an organization you're interested in and get that informational interview scheduled. Here are a few tips on how to win over your informational interviewer:

- Have a compelling story about your life to share with your interviewer.
- Apply what you learn in Chapter IV about developing your soft skills.
- Have a question to ask after the interview is over (e.g., Would it be okay if we connected on LinkedIn? May I reach out if I have any questions?).
- Do research on the interviewee so that you're prepared to ask good questions about her career.
- If you're an introvert and tend to be more on the reserved side, practice your interview skills with friends and family.

Later in this chapter, I cover how to find the right people for informational interviews and ways to craft your message.

Online Is Great, Offline Is Greater

The truth is, online dating is a great way to meet people. You can read a person's profile, view photos, and get a good sense of who someone is (if they're honest) in a few short minutes. If a person strikes your interest, it's easy enough to message them and if they reciprocate, engage in conversation. However, as we all know, in order to take the relationship to the next level, to really get to know someone, you have to meet in real life. The same can be said about networking.

Back when I was in college and throughout my first few years in the civilian workforce, there was no meaningful social media. There were the very beginnings of social media but not with the networking capabilities we have today. If we wanted to grow our networks, we did so at live events. We squeezed out of our comfort zones, met in person, and built real life relationships. Then as social networks like LinkedIn and Twitter became mainstream, online networking increased in popularity.

However, in my experience, online networking on its own is shallow in nature. There's only so far a relationship can go through private messages, video, e-mail, and Tweets. Furthermore, people are inundated with online messages, so the longer you wait to take the relationship offline, the greater the chance that the relationship will fizzle out—similar to online dating. There must be an offline component to make a relationship meaningful. Don't be afraid to ask people in your network to meet for a cup of coffee. If you're both finding value in the relationship you've built online, you shouldn't face much friction taking it offline.

While you're in college, explore the vast amount of in-person networking opportunities available to you. Yes, take advantage of online networking. However, complement it with attending local events or setting in-person meetings, and build those relationships in real life.

How to Build a Professional Online Network

The philosophy of building a professional online network is fairly straightforward. It consists of finding people who fit your professional criteria, connecting with them on various social networks, and building relationships through genuine social engagement. Let's walk through an example of how to find relevant professionals on social media (in this case, Twitter) in a manner that could possibly lead to personal connection and certainly would lead to being more informed about the goings-on in your field of choice. Let's say you're a marketing major hoping to work within a nonprofit organization (though this will be applicable to any professional goal).

TOOLS NEEDED:

- Twitter Account: While many use Twitter to catch up on the news and celebrity gossip, you'll learn how to use it to build your professional network.

- LinkedIn Account: In addition to using LinkedIn to discover job opportunities, you will use it to meet and connect with people you want in your network.

- Followerwonk: This tool allows you to search Twitter accounts and find relevant people to add to your network.

  - Note: As of September 1, 2016, Followerwonk is up for acquisition. Features, functionality, name, and pricing may change post sale.

- TweetDeck: This tool is owned by Twitter. Tweet-Deck allows you to follow multiple streams of Twitter conversations, which is important for network building.

- Crystal Knows: This tool provides communication recommendations in both style and substance for each person you reach out to include in your network.

Twitter Strategy

How to Search Twitter for the Most Relevant Contacts

STEP 1: IDENTIFY PROFESSIONALS WORKING IN VIABLE NONPROFIT ORGANIZATIONS

1. Sign up for an account with Followerwonk.com. Subscriptions are billed monthly, and there are no annual commitments. There is also a free trial, so you might want to give that a try first. In the worst case, pay for the first month and then cancel.

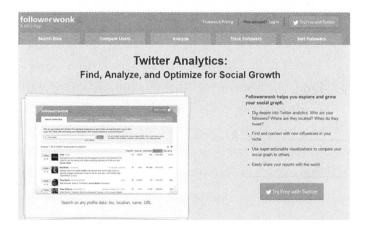

2. Once signed in to Followerwonk, click on the first tab, "Search Bios."

3. Below the search bar, click on the "more options" link.

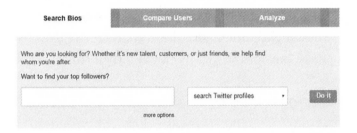

4. Enter the keyword "nonprofit" into the search bar.
5. If you'd prefer to keep the search specific to a certain geographic range, you can do so in the "Location" field.
6. Once you've entered your search criteria, click the orange "Do it" button.

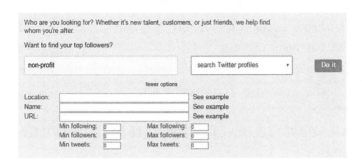

7. If you've done this correctly, you'll find approximately 50,000 Twitter accounts that meet the criteria you entered.

8. From here, you can sort the data table based on whatever criteria you wish.

9. Start clicking the follow button next to the names that you wish to connect with.

STEP 2: ADD "FOLLOWED" ACCOUNTS TO A PRIVATE TWITTER LIST

1. Log into your Twitter account.
2. Navigate to "Lists."
3. On the right-hand side of the screen, click the "Create new list" button.

4. Create a list name.

5. Enter a description that will help you differentiate between the various lists you create.

6. Select the "private" radio box in the Privacy section. This will keep people from knowing you've added them to a list.

7. Finally click on "Save list."

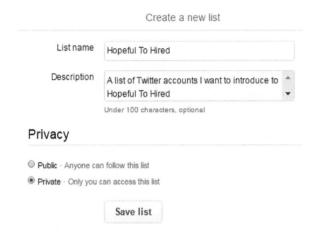

8. Once you've created your list, you'll find a "Find people to add to your list" search bar.

9. Start adding the Twitter accounts that you've followed in Followerwonk.

10. Once you've completed this step, you now have a solid list of possible connections to build relationships with.

STEP 3: LISTEN TO TWITTER LISTS THROUGH TWEETDECK

Listening is the most important aspect of connecting with people on social media. You can gain a lot of insight about people by paying attention to what they share. It's no different than sitting at a table with a group of people. The more you listen to what people share about themselves, the more you learn. Active listening makes you much more effective in connecting and building out your network.

1. TweetDeck is a Twitter platform owned by Twitter. Simply visit tweetdeck.com, connect your Twitter account, and log in.

2. In the far left column on the screen, click on the
   "+ Add Column" button.

3. On the left-hand side of the "Choose column type"
   pop-up, click the "Lists" button.

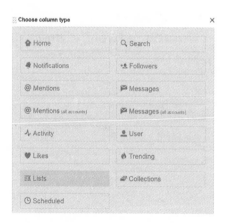

4. Select the list(s) that you've created from your Fol-lowerwonk research.

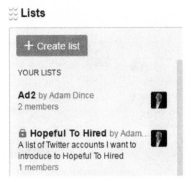

5. Click "Add Column."

6. Once completed, you'll find your Twitter list(s) appearing on the far right column on the dashboard.
7. From here, you can listen to what your list members are Tweeting.

STEP 4: RESPOND TO TWITTER LISTS THROUGH TWEETDECK

In the soft skills section of *Hopeful to Hired*, I shared Will Rogers's quote, "You never get a second chance to make a good first impression." You don't want to jump the gun and be too forward with your messaging as that can easily come off as too aggressive or exploitative. The key is to be patient and wait for the right opportunities to reach out. I highly recommend the following approach:

1. Start interacting with your Twitter list contacts by retweeting the content they share that resonates with you.
2. Feel free to Tweet to your list contacts and let them know that you're enjoying their content. Just be careful not to overdo it here. It could be seen as annoying. Use your best judgment.
3. Build a friendly rapport over time.

BUILD COMMUNITY THROUGH ATTENDING TWITTER CHATS

Twitter is by far my favorite social network. It's my go-to place for reading breaking news, finding industry-related articles, and participating in targeted chats. Nicole M. Miller (@nmillerbrooks) gives a good definition of Twitter chats:

> A Twitter chat is where a group of Twitter users meet at a predetermined time to discuss a certain topic, using a designated hashtag (#) for each tweet contributed. A host or moderator will pose questions (designated with Q1, Q2 . . .) to prompt responses from participants (using A1, A2 . . .) and encourage interaction among the group. Chats typically last an hour.[16]

Participating in Twitter chats gives you the opportunity to meet like-minded people, build your network, and showcase your smarts. Twitter chats also provide a great medium for building relationships that stretch far past Twitter. I've met some of my closest friends

16   Nicole Miller, "A Step-by-Step Guide To Hosting or Joining a Twitter Chat," Buffer Blog, August 20, 2014, https://blog.bufferapp.com/twitter-chat-101.

and industry contacts through Twitter chats.

The first step, of course, is to find a few chats to attend. If you Google "Twitter chat schedules," you'll find a list of resources to help you find some chats that could be relevant. Take a quick look at the Tweet Report Schedule on tweetreports.com as an example. Once you start attending a chat or two, you'll find that chatters are members of many chats. If you're following those people, they'll help you discover other chats that you might be interested in joining.

As you begin to attend Twitter chats, you want to make sure that in addition to answering the questions that the moderator asks, you're building relationships. In order to build meaningful relationships, proper etiquette is required. Here are my golden Twitter chat etiquette tips:

- Be yourself: Let your hair down and have some fun. As you may have noticed, people can be way too dry on Twitter. Don't be afraid to let your personality show.

- Be creative: Where appropriate, include imagery to illustrate your points. GIFs, Memes, etc. In doing so, use humor when needed, but remember to keep it professional.

- Be conversational: Spend as much time responding to other people's answers as you do answering questions.

- Connect: Follow people who you interact with—they'll most likely follow back.
- Be gracious: At the end of chats, thank the host and connect. Hosts put a lot of time into building and running their Twitter chats. Showing gratitude goes a long way.
- Keep in contact: Keep your TweetDeck open, and keep the conversation going throughout the week.
- Share: Share Twitter chat community content (if it's good), and don't hesitate to share yours with them.

Twitter is a meaningful network for connecting with new people. Twitter is also a fantastic starting point to start a relationship before moving to other more professional networks like LinkedIn.

LinkedIn Strategy
Expanded From Twitter

Let's continue to build upon what we did with Twitter on LinkedIn. While Twitter is my favorite social network, not everyone shares that sentiment. Many of the accounts that you discover through Followerwonk and Twitter chats may be more active on other networks. Most professionals are active or at least present on LinkedIn. So it makes sense as a natural progression to take relationships from Twitter to LinkedIn. Here are some tips:

1. When it feels right, connect on LinkedIn with the contacts you've developed relationships with on Twitter.
2. Write a warm contact request to those you're requesting to connect with.
3. Be personable and engage with your new LinkedIn contacts.
4. Ask for informational interviews. After exchanging a few messages with your LinkedIn contacts, ask politely if he or she would be available for an informational interview. We'll discuss more about the technicalities of how to

reach out to contacts later in the chapter.

5. Show sincere gratitude for any advice, help, or mentorship provided. Thank-yous go a long way.

LINKEDIN SEARCH

The search functionality that LinkedIn provides is fantastic. Think of businesses or brands you'd like to work for or industries you're interested in working in. Spend time doing research, and use your findings as your search criteria. Let's continue with the example of finding professionals that work in nonprofit organizations.

1. Once you're on LinkedIn.com, you'll find its search box at the very top of each page.
2. Just to the right of the blue magnifying glass icon, click the "Advanced" link.
3. In the "Keywords" field, enter "nonprofit."
4. Enter data into any of the other fields present on the far left side of the screen to refine your search.
5. Finally, in the center of the page, you'll find other potential variables that you might want to select in order to finalize your search criteria.
6. To add connections, visit the profiles of people you

wish to connect with and click the blue "connect" button.

7. Reach out to those you're interested in connecting with. In the next section I introduce you to Crystal. Crystal is a tool that analyzes LinkedIn profiles and provides both substantive and stylistic recommendations to craft your communication unique to each person you wish to communicate with.

LINKEDIN GROUPS

Essentially, LinkedIn Groups are communities where people with similar interests and passions come together to share information and build relationships. If you're looking at LinkedIn profiles of people you wish to connect with, you can easily find which groups they belong to and also join. Below is a screenshot of the "Groups" section of my LinkedIn profile.

Joining groups that prospective contacts belong to will provide you with an opportunity to network in a more informal setting before requesting a LinkedIn connection. Additionally, I've found LinkedIn Groups to be a powerful tool to meet likeminded people in my industry. As a college student, you can use Groups to find people in the industry that you're interested in adding to your professional network.

You can also find Groups to join without looking at a LinkedIn profile. There are many types of LinkedIn Groups that would serve you well. The easiest way to find a comprehensive list of available LinkedIn Groups is through Google.

Once you click on the link above, you'll find a plethora of Groups listed alphabetically. Use this page to start finding groups to participate in.

Again, be strategic about how you use LinkedIn Groups. Be a part of the conversation, be helpful, show genuine interest in others, and connect appropriately. Additionally, once you connect with professionals on LinkedIn, you'll have an opportunity to build those relationships outside of Groups.

Meet Crystal
The Web Application

Your communication style will influence the way others interpret your personal brand. Before you start engaging with professionals, do your research. Oftentimes, I get formal letter messages from students that want to connect. I ignore those. However, I always respond to the students that reach out with a well-thought-out personalized message.

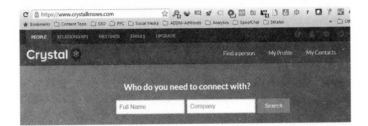

CrystalKnows.com is an intelligent tool that will coach you through the communication process. In this section, I will illustrate how it works and how to use it. I can tell you from experience that Crystal will make your online communication much more effective. By the way, Crystal offers a free membership that will provide much of the information you'll need to write and construct a well-informed personalized message. After signing up and logging into CrystalKnows.com:

1. Enter the person's name and business name in the text boxes.

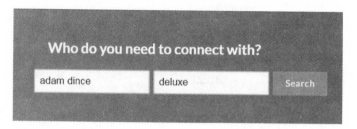

2. Click "Search."
3. Crystal will return a list of people that match your search criteria.
4. Click on the person you're searching for.

5. Get familiar with and take notes on the profile information given across the top tabs.

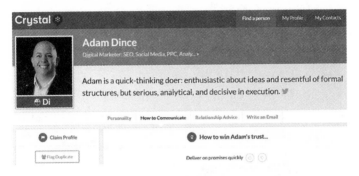

6. Use that information to construct your messaging.

Meet the Crystal Chrome Plug-In

If you're using Google Chrome, Crystal provides a helpful extension that allows you to leverage the Crystal within Gmail, Twitter, LinkedIn, etc. . . .native on each site. To implement the Crystal extension, visit the Chrome Web Store and search "Crystal."

Once you've implemented the extension, start experimenting with how to use it:

CRYSTAL + GMAIL:

1. Open up Gmail.
2. Click on the "Compose Message" button.
3. Enter the e-mail address of the person to whom you'll be sending information.
4. To the right of the blue "Send" button at the bottom of the message box, click on the gray "Select Person" button.

5. Enter the information of the person to whom you're writing.

6. Select the person, screenshot the profile pop-up box, and close the pop-up box.

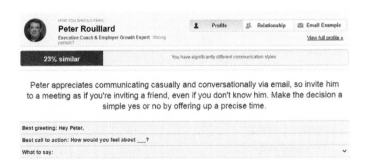

7. Refer to the profile screenshot to help personalize your message.

8. Notice that the gray button that used to read "Select Person" is now green. The text in the green button will change as you construct your message.

9. Also, on the right-hand side of the Gmail screen, you'll find a Crystal profile box that will help you craft an appropriate message to your contact.

10. Click on the "Select an e-mail template" drop-down box.

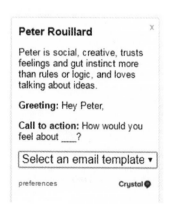

11. Once you select a proper e-mail template type, Crystal will present you a template to work from.

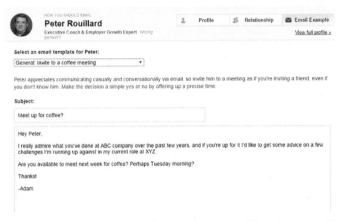

12. Make sure to customize and personalize the e-mail template prior to sending.

CRYSTAL + LINKEDIN:

In the previous section, I illustrated how to use Crystal with Gmail. In this section, I will highlight Crystal's functionality within LinkedIn.

1. Visit LinkedIn.com.
2. Open up a person's profile.
3. Right below the person's summary toward the top of the screen, you'll find a Crystal box that will

highlight what you need to know about the person.

4. Pay special attention to the keywords and phrases that Crystal provides.

Key words and phrases to use with Peter...

"I appreciate you for..."   "How do you feel about..."   Make jokes

Colorful, descriptive words   "Don't forget..."   "I'll send a reminder"

Bold claims   Personal questions   "Reminds me of the time when..."

"Let's chat"

When speaking to Peter...

Tell a few jokes

Use self-deprecating humor (don't act like you take yourself too seriously)

Talk about abstract philosophies or ideas   Emphasize the future

When emailing Peter...

Use emotionally expressive language   Appeal to his feelings to drive him to action

Use an emoticon :)   Write with short casual language and abbreviations

When working with Peter...

Recognize his achievements verbally   Express criticism in person or on the phone

Send a reminder the day before a meeting

Schedule meetings casually (i.e. tomorrow afternoon)

TWITTER:

1. Visit Twitter.com.
2. Open up a person's profile.
3. Find the "View Personality" button underneath the profile description and click it.

Adam Dince
@AdamDince

Director, Earned Media @DeluxeCorp
(#SEO, #SocialMedia #ContentStrategy)
@StKateMBA. Views mine. #Speaker
#Blogger #SpoofChat co-creator.

View personality

Minneapolis, MN
adamdince.com
Joined April 2008

4. Post-click, you'll find potential matches. Click the correct option.

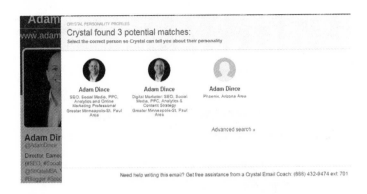

5. Post-click, Crystal will provide a profile description.

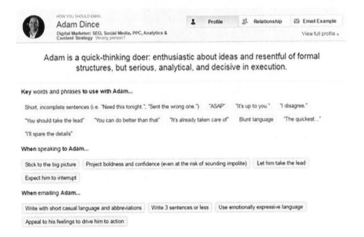

6. Use the insights Crystal provides to help construct your message.

Crystal's integration with LinkedIn can help you craft a much more powerful message than if you'd simply attempted one on your own.

Attend In-Person Networking Events

A few days ago, I had the opportunity to conduct a group informational interview at a local university. I asked the marketing and advertising students, who were less than a month away from graduation, if they had jobs lined up. None of them did. I then asked if they had networks to build a pool of prospective resources to reach out to. None of them did. My last question was whether or not they belonged to any of the local professional associations or organizations. Guess what the response was. Take it one step further: none of them knew these organizations existed.

One of the gravest mistakes that many of us (not just students) make is that we solely focus our network prospecting online. While online networking can pay major dividends, in-person events can net better results much faster.

In-person networking allows others to get a better sense of who we are and vice versa. The nonverbal communication that happens in person can take us much further than messages we send across the web.

So much positive bonding happens in person that just can't happen online.

A few years ago, I mentored Katherine, a student that wanted to break into the digital advertising profession. When I asked her if she'd ever attended an industry event, Katherine mentioned that she had, but only events that were sponsored by her school. I invited her to join me at a local industry event where there would be an abundance of hiring managers and influencers. I thought it would be a great opportunity to introduce her to people who might be able to help once she graduated.

It didn't take long before Katherine started approaching the professionals in attendance. She left with cards, LinkedIn connections, and a few people also agreed to give informational interviews. What Katherine was able to accomplish in two short hours at an in-person event would have taken her weeks, if not months, online.

In 2015, the local AdFed chapter in Minneapolis asked me to be a mentor at a "speed-dating" networking event for college students. A student, who was just about to graduate from the University of Minnesota, joined me at my table and introduced herself. Ashlyn shared that she had attended the event because she knew I would be there and that she'd just applied at Deluxe (where I worked at the time) for an entry-level job in my department. We ended up chatting for a good twenty minutes. I loved her personality and was impressed by her ambition. Ashlyn was able to clearly articulate why she wanted the role she had applied for. She also described, in detail, why she felt Deluxe was the right company for her. The next morning, I walked over to the hiring manager's desk and gave Ashlyn a glowing review. I shared some of what Ashlyn and I had discussed at the event. To make a long story short, Ashlyn's been at Deluxe for a year and a half now and is doing an outstanding job. That being said, once we've connected with people in person, we must bring those relationships online to continue building.

When you meet people at in-person events, make sure to connect with them afterward on LinkedIn or another network we discussed earlier in the chapter. And don't simply connect—continue building the relationships you started in person. When connections share things like articles or professional, it's easy enough to like, comment, or share. It's easy enough to congratulate connections on work anniversaries and promotions. It's also simple to see if people in your network have connections with companies you're interested in interning or working for. Finally, as you publish and/or share content on LinkedIn (which you should be doing), your connections will have the opportunity to engage with you.

Also, avoid moving relationships offline to online and not reconnecting in person again. Once you've made that in-person connection, make sure you foster it by periodically checking in. Additionally, if you're building meaningful online relationships, you may get the opportunity to meet those folks at these networking events.

A few in-person networking options:
- Campus organizations
- Meetup.com
- Career fairs
- Professional organizations (typically student pricing is available)
- Conferences (typically student pricing is available)
- Shareholder meetings (see "Other Pro Tips" a few sections down)

Network on Company Blog Posts

Here's a stealth tip that can help you make a contact at a brand you're interested in working for. Let's use

BuzzFeed as an example.

1. Visit company blog (Buzzfeed: BF Blog).
2. Click on any article.
3. Let's look at this article written by Claire Moses:

Follow on Facebook to upgrade your home and life >

Behind The Scenes Of The BuzzFeed News Newsletter

This is what goes into creating a daily news newsletter product for an international audience.

posted on Apr 4, 2016, at 11:28 a.m.

Claire Moses
Editor, News Curation

Every day, around 8 a.m. EST — early in L.A., lunch time in the UK — we send out the BuzzFeed News newsletter. Here are some of our most reliable tips and tricks.

Journalism 101: The same rules apply.

Every week day, we ask ourselves "Who, what, where, when, and why?" The *why* is both the most interesting and the most difficult question to answer. This is also where our regular features like "**what's next,**" "**a bit of background,**" and "**a little extra**" come in — to expand on that *why*.

4. Scroll down to the comments section at the bottom of the article.
5. Notice that there are no comments present.

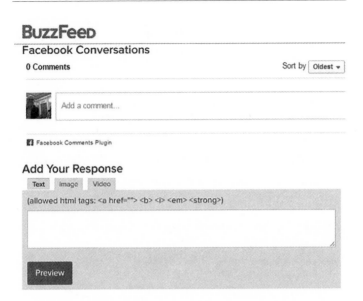

As I write this section, the article referenced in the above screenshot is four weeks old yet has no blog engagement. What if you were the hero who read the article and asked a really good question? What if you started a conversation with the author in the comments area? What if you asked the author if he or she would be willing to connect on LinkedIn or Twitter?

Keep in mind that you are in a highly competitive marketplace. The best way to become a top job prospect coming out of college is by doing a lot of the legwork while still in college. Blog comments and discussions are a great way to connect with influential people at a multitude of brands that you're interested in working for.

Build a Google Resume

A Google resume refers to the findable content about you on search engines' results pages. If you Google "Adam Dince" the collection of results is my Google resume. Building a Google resume requires you to put yourself out there, online.

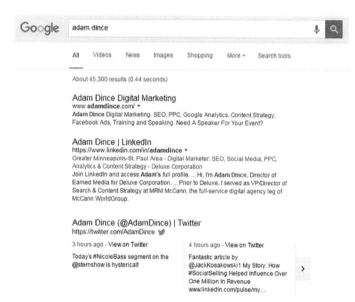

After a speaking engagement at a local college, a student pulled me aside and asked for a few moments of my time. With frustration in his voice, he told me that there was so much more to him than what appears on his resume or LinkedIn profile. He asked me what I recommend he do to paint a more complete picture of himself when applying for an internship. I asked him what appeared in his Google search results when he searched his name. He didn't know.

Believe it or not, hiring managers want to know more about you than your professional and educational experience. However, as Troy mentioned in the Foreword, we just don't have the time to bring in each applicant for a discovery session. This is why having a meaningful Google resume is important. So how do you build a Google resume?

#1 TURN YOUR NAME INTO A DOMAIN NAME

Own your name! For example, I own mine: www. adamdince.com. Registering a domain name is both cheap and easy. Here are few options for domain name registrars:

- GoDaddy.com
- NetworkSolutions.com
- Register.com

Keep in mind, the more common your name, the harder it may be to get an exact match for a domain name. If this is the case, consider doing one of the following:

- Include a middle initial (www.adamsdince. com)
- Choose a different domain extension (www. adamdince.net)
- Add a location (www.adamdinceminnesota. com)
- Add a desired profession (www.adamdincemarketer.com)

Note: none of the above domain names are active, so no need to visit them.

#2 BUILD A WEBSITE

When you register your domain name with a provider, they may offer a variety of website solutions. For instance, GoDaddy offers a WordPress solution for a low annual cost. If you're looking for a free solution, I recommend checking out options like WordPress. com, Wix, and Web.com.

#3 TELL YOUR STORY ON YOUR SITE

A personal website is the perfect place to tell your story.

Make sure you include the following pages:

- Homepage: The homepage will most likely be the page that returns in search engine results when your name is searched. Think of the homepage as the front page of a magazine. Don't clutter it up with content. Make sure to be interesting, succinct, and visually appealing (many free providers have nice templates).

- About Me: This is your chance to tell your story. What do you want a prospective employer to know about you? Think about the soft skills chapter where we talked about how to use your personality type and strengths to talk about who you are. Do you have hobbies? Passions? Have an interesting volunteer experience to talk about? Be creative here. Creativity rules!

- Resume: Another chance to list your resume and potentially add some flare to it. For example, sharing your resume through video format can be powerful, and it can highlight your communication skills and ability to leverage technology to your advantage.

- Dream Job: I recommend including a page that talks about the type of role you want and company you want to work for. If it's a specific company, make sure to mention them specifically. For instance, if you're dream is to work as an accountant for Google, be clear about it on this page.

- Portfolio: If you've worked on projects throughout your undergraduate program that are relevant to your career focus, this is your opportunity to showcase them to potential employers.

- Organizational Memberships: List the different organizations you're involved with. As we spoke about in the "Attend In-Person Networking Events" section, there are a variety of organizations you can join. Showing employers that you are active in professional communities can go a long way in building your credibility.

- Blog: This is your chance to showcase your thought leadership. If you're a marketing major, you can write about channels like social media, paid search advertising, SEO, e-mail marketing, etc. If you're an English major, you can post in-depth book review articles. Be creative here. Know that prospective employers will appreciate the effort you put in, and this will provide them a better idea of how you think.
- Link to your public social media profiles (e.g., LinkedIn, Twitter, Instagram, etc.). Make connecting easy!

#4 OPTIMIZE YOUR PUBLIC SOCIAL MEDIA PROFILES

If your social media profiles are set to public (not private), search engines will be able to access and read all of the available content. In return, if you've optimized your public social media profiles you'll have a great opportunity for those profiles to be found in search results. As an example, Google "Adam Dince," and you'll see many of my social profiles.

Think of which social profiles are most relevant to your career and focus on those first. For example, Google is now returning Tweets in search results. Tweets tend to be returned if the Twitter profile is optimized and if there is enough activity to warrant Twitter results. For the purposes of this book, we'll look at Twitter and LinkedIn as the social profiles to properly optimize.

TWITTER

- Account Name: Should be your name (e.g., twitter.com/adamdince). By abbreviating your name or using some other pseudonym (e.g., twitter.com/marketingguru), you're hurting your chances of returning in search results. Also, refer to domain name recommendations (Step 1) if your name is already taken in Twitter.
- Name: Use your real name. Don't abbreviate or use your middle name as your last.
- Description: Make sure it reads as professional. Do include any organizations you're a part of (e.g., Member #PRSAA) and other relevant hashtags.
- Location: Please be accurate here. If a hiring manager is looking for someone in your geographical area and you've listed "Somewhere on earth" as your location, you may not return. In my case, I list "Minneapolis, MN."
- Website: Do link to your website. This will help the major search engines and prospective employ-

ers find your website faster. The sooner engines find your site, the faster you'll be eligible to return.

- Be creative: Check out twitter.com/adamdince

and see what I did with my header. I wanted to tell a story that best represents who I am. For graphics, I highly recommend Canva.com. Canva is a free tool where you can create graphics for most of your social profiles.

- Pin a relevant Tweet: Twitter allows users to pin a Tweet so that it always shows up first when your profile is viewed. Pick a Tweet that best represents you. Maybe you've Tweeted a link to your personal website. Again, be creative here!

Getting Google to return your LinkedIn profile in its search results is fairly easy. Just make sure that your:

- Name is spelled properly when you set up your account
- Name is present in the URL (e.g., www.linkedin.com/in/adamdince)
- Location is correct

However, optimization is more than appearing in search results. Remember, when employers find your profile, you'll want to ensure that you are telling them the best possible story about who you are. Here are some areas to focus on.

1. Publish articles on LinkedIn Pulse (linkedin. com/pulse).

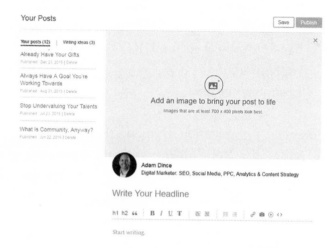

Remember, prospective hiring managers will be reading your content, so keep it professional and relevant to the type of job or career path you're pursuing.

2. Within your profile summary, you can include videos, images, documents, or presentations. Use this area to include any relevant work or research.

Summary

Hi, I'm Adam Dince, Director of Earned Media for Deluxe Corporation. I manage a team of enterprise SEO, social media and content strategists across a wide variety of verticals.

Prior to Deluxe, I served as VP/Director of Search & Content Strategy at MRM McCann, the full-service digital agency leg of McCann WorldGroup.

I've amassed over fourteen years of internet...

Getting past the 100% Not Provided Googl...

MN SEO's Hangout with Rand Fishkin of M...

What's Up With Search, S...

3. List all volunteer experience in the "Volunteer" section. As a new graduate, you may not have much experience to highlight. Volunteering is an activity that will show prospective employers that you not only care about giving back to the community, but it also tells them what sorts of orga-

nizations you support. In other words, it helps tell more about you than what you might ordinarily list on your resume.

Volunteer

Math Buddy

Mounds View Public Schools

October 2013 – Present (2 years 8 months) | Education

Math tutor and buddy for fifth grade students at Island Lake Elementary School.

4. List all certifications that you've earned in the "Certifications" section. As you'll read more about in the "Two Final Tips" section of this chapter, one of the things you can do while still in school is to start getting certified. For instance, if you know that a meaningful portion of your job will be administrative, pursue a certification like the Microsoft Office Specialist (MOS). As you complete certifications, list them here. This is not a section to be overlooked.

Certifications

Inbound Marketing Certified
HubSpot
March 2014 – March 2015

Certified Social Ambassador
Deluxe Corporation
Starting October 2013

DELUXE

Inbound Certification
HubSpot
April 2015 – May 2016

Google AdWords Certified
Google
August 2015 – August 2016

G

Google Analytics Individual Qualification (IQ)
Google
November 2015 – May 2017

G

5. List any organizations you're involved with in the "Organizations" section. One of the most important things you can do while in school is join organizations and then take leadership positions. Think back to my Phi Theta Kappa story earlier in the book. One of the benefits of joining and being active in an organization is that it allows you to speak to your abilities and how you've applied them during school. Look to join organizations

that give you the best story to tell potential employers.

Organizations

SocialMedia.org
Red Council
May 2013 – May 2014

MIMA - Minnesota Interactive Marketing Association
Starting December 2014

6. If you volunteer for a nonprofit organization, ask the volunteer coordinator or other leadership for a recommendation. If you're working your way through school, whether on or off campus, make sure to ask your supervisor for a recommendation. While your college job duties might not be relevant to your future pursuits, the quality of work, leadership, and attitude you have are important for future employers to know about.

Director of Earned Media - SB (SEO, Social, Content Strategy)
Deluxe Corporation

Tim Carroll
Senior Vice President eCommerce and Digital Marketing at Arrowhead Electrical Products

❝ Adam would consider it an insult if I called him a guru, so I won't. That being he said, he is whatever word you use to describe someone who is very very very good at what they do. Adam has an infectious enthusiasm for online marketing and he is equal parts student and teacher. He also is a wonderful networker... regardless of the problem, Adam always "knows someone" who... **more** ❞

February 23, 2016, Tim managed Adam at Deluxe Corporation

7. Make sure that your profile photo is professional.

Other Social Profile Best Practices

Social networks are supposed to be safe places where we can be ourselves. However, as mentioned earlier, if a search engine can access the content on your social profiles, your prospective employers, mentors, etc. can too. If you're going to use any of your social profiles for things you wouldn't want employers to see, make sure to set those accounts to private. Keep in mind, some employers ask prospective employees for access to their private social media accounts. While more states are making this practice illegal, it's still legal in some areas of the country.

On your public profiles, you want to put your best foot forward. Here are some tips to consider:

- It's okay if your profile photos on Twitter, Facebook, Pinterest, Instagram, Snapchat, Snapcode, and other social media sites are not professional. In fact, social media is meant to showcase your personality. However, avoid using profile photos that are inappropriate. If you're unsure about whether your profile photos are appropriate, ask your on-campus career center, friends, family, and network.

- Avoid heated topics like political and religious discussions. Yes, many of us have political views, and it's okay to share them on private profiles. However, throughout your career, you're going to work with and for people who have different views. Posting partisan or off-color political comments that the public can view could cause you to miss out on a potential job opportunity.

- Avoid the party pics. Yes, we all love to go out and have a good time. And you may end up partying with your future employers and mentors. Lord knows I've partied with mine. However, keep in mind that your public social profiles may be the first impression a prospective employer or mentor has of you. No need to give them any false positives about who you are as a person.

- Avoid posting things about relationship drama. If you're sharing about an engagement or a fun weekend with your significant other, fine. However, if you've been scorned and are heartbroken, consider saving that for your private networks. Also, avoid posting the make-out pictures on public profiles.

- Keep health issues private. While we want to keep our friends and family informed about our health conditions, we don't necessarily want our employers to know.

Two Final Tips

Now that you've made it through "Networking With a Purpose" and "Building a Google Resume," let's finish this chapter up with a few final tips.

BUY A SHARE OF STOCK IN A COMPANY YOU ARE INTERESTED IN WORKING FOR

In some cases, you may follow all of the recommendations provided in *Hopeful to Hired* yet still find it hard to get your foot in the door with the right person. A classmate in my MBA program recently landed a job she really wanted and shared how she did it.

Simply purchasing a single share of stock in the publicly traded company she wanted to work for allowed her to attend shareholder meetings. When she attended the shareholder meetings, she was able to network with the right people and ended up with a job offer.

GET PROFESSIONALLY CERTIFIED

A professional certification can help you stand out against the competition. A college student with professional certifications comes off as more ambitious, driven, and focused than his peers. There are certifications you can earn while still in college. If you're majoring in an advertising or marketing area, consider getting Google AdWords and Google Analytics certifications. At the very least, get Google Analytics certified. Both certifications are free!

Additionally, every industry uses software or Software as a Service (SaaS) to manage the heavy lifting. If you're an accounting major, you might use Quick-Books. Engineering majors, you may use CAD on the job. Review a meaningful sample of job descriptions related to your major, look for common software familiarities required, and attempt to get certified prior to graduation. Being familiar with and certified in necessary software makes you a far more attractive entry-level candidate for most jobs across a variety of industries.

LISTEN TO THE PROS

T hus far in *Hopeful to Hired*, I've provided you with the strategies, tactics, and tips that I give to students whom I mentor. In this chapter, I will share insights from a few veteran professionals whom I greatly admire. Each of the four people included in this chapter speak from a wealth of experience. I asked each of the professionals to respond to these two questions:

- *What did you do in college to prepare yourself for landing your first job in your area of study?*

- *What advice do you have for college students preparing to start looking for their first job in industry?*

David Hohman

EVP, Global Client Business Partner,
Agency Solutions, The Nielsen Company

From Boots to Suits: My Transition from the Military to a Civilian Career

When I decided to separate from the Marine Corps, I thought long and hard about what I wanted to do, where I wanted to live, and whether or not my military experience would translate to the corporate world. I had completed my Bachelor's degree in finance while on active duty, but I was concerned that the experiences I had in the Marine Corps would not be seen as relevant to a corporate HR director or hiring manager. How could I communicate my strengths and abilities so that hiring managers could understand my worth? In speaking with many service members who contemplate this transition, I have come to realize that it is a very common concern, but at the time I felt I was alone.

I soon realized that I needed a plan to be successful, and the first step was to assemble all of the information a prospective employer might want to see. Think of it as your personal career catalog—your experience, training, accomplishments, personal information, military record, etc. In mine I collected the following documents:

Military Service:
- Separation papers, DD 214
- Training record
- Honors and awards
- Service record
- Security clearance
- Medical record

Personal Identification:
- Birth certificate
- Proof of citizenship
- Social security card
- Passport
- Photo ID

Work Experience:
- Work history (job titles, dates, duties, accomplishments, awards)
- Work samples
- Honors and citations
- Community activities
- References

Education & Training:
- Transcripts
- Diplomas/Certificates
- Honors
- Licenses/Certifications

Next I identified my personal network, people who would be willing to help me in my job search. I started with military friends and peers, both those who had separated and those still serving. Some were valuable references, while others were helpful by telling me what worked and didn't work in their job searches. If you are returning to your hometown, reconnecting with people from school or work is a good start. While you are still on active duty, you can begin to build your civilian network through LinkedIn and its interest groups, Twitter, alumni organizations, and professional associations too. This will help you learn more about civilian opportunities and find people to help you to the right job or career.

While the military is a very supportive organization, the reality is that once you've made the decision to separate, it can feel like you are on your own. I knew I would need help in making this transition successfully, so I started with people I knew and respected, many of whom had military experience—my father, my godfather, parents of friends, etc. Then I wrote letters, lots of letters, asking for their help and advice. This is a critical early step—building your network. You would be surprised at how many people want to help. I didn't ask for a job, I asked them for advice. I asked what qualities they were looking for in potential candidates for employment in their career fields, the qualities and experiences they valued, and professional associations and organizations that could provide more information.

Once you have defined your initial contact list, define your goals. Don't just go to events, send letters and e-mail, or have coffee with friends and call it networking. Define what you need, what you offer, and what you will do in fairly specific terms. You want quality connections for mutual benefit. Think about what you want to learn from each contact, what you will share about yourself, what kind of help you want—be specific—company info, references, referrals, whom you will ask for introductions and to whom they should introduce you. Talk to people in the career field you are interested in. Ask them what changes, obstacles, and opportunities they see. Ask them what keeps them up at night. Be courteous and interested, and thank them for their time.

Jorie Waterman

VP, Customer Acquisition and Internet Marketing at Shutterfly Inc.

What did you do in college to prepare yourself for landing your first job in your area of study?

I have always followed great ideas, whether it was before college, in college, and in my career. Great ideas, or at least ideas that I love(d), enabled me to be inspired by the work I did and ultimately propelled me forward in my career. Even my major at Harvard, Buddhism, was unconventional and enabled me to understand more about how people make decisions and what motivates them. This ended up being a great introduction to the advertising industry. I learned how to think in college and how to ask questions, and both skills have served me well as I have followed my passion around the country and the world.

What advice do you have for college students preparing to look for their first job in an industry?

Follow your passion. If you love the work you are doing, you will be much more successful than if you go into a line of work that doesn't inspire you.

Approach your work and your workmates with respect, transparency, and honesty.

Learn the basics of the industry before you jump in—look for internships, look for training available online, talk to people.

Chris Marquardt
Senior Partner, Maxus Global Media

What did you do in college to prepare yourself for landing your first job in your area of study?

It would be inaccurate to say that the studies I pursued in college were the result of careful calculation and a clear idea of the career I would chase after graduation, but it's also fair to say that four years of taking very different classes—whatever I thought would be interesting— was good preparation for life and a career in interactive consulting. In hindsight my choice of career focus stemmed from the very same desire to take classes across the liberal arts rather than to focus on one field in particular. But this doesn't lead me to the conclusion that a broad education is right for everyone, rather that the essential element to success, or at least continued interest in the daily grind, is an ongoing excitement for the work.

Like a lot of college students, I did not spend my years of study with a clear understanding of what I should do with the rest of my life. Instead I was happy to be relatively free of expectations and to follow my curiosity, and in this way I was very lucky. I loved the broad interplay of art, technology, and sociology across history and was glad to take courses across disciplines. It took a few years of working in law firms before I discovered connected computing and found the job that could unite so many areas of study into one career. So I unwittingly had a pretty good curriculum for interactive marketing and strategy—but I certainly could have saved some time getting there if I had asked myself the right questions during college, many of which Adam has covered and answered in *Hopeful to Hired*.

What should college students a year or two away from graduation start doing now to prepare for landing their first job?

It's never too early to assess what you're studying and doing outside of classes that keeps your focus and interest. If you can be honest with yourself about what you like doing day in and day out, you're halfway there.

Then the task is to understand the roles that interest you. There's no reward for shyness here. Use every connection you have—most schools do a great job of connecting students to alumni in a chosen field—and meet everyone. Be open about what interests you, and ask a lot of questions. It's the only way to develop the understanding you need to go into a new job with your eyes open—and make it last.

Jac White

CEO, Savoteur (Daily Secret)

What did you do in college to prepare yourself for landing your first job in your area of study?

Thankfully, I went to school in a city (NYC) where interning was possible during my school semester. I took full advantage of the opportunity to work part time in a related field while I was still in school. I graduated with real experience and a resume I was proud of. I was also involved in extracurricular activities at school. I worked at the health clinic to promote the free services we provided to students, organizing on-campus festivals or giveaways. Internships, work experience, and extracurricular activities are all things I look for on a resume, especially for employees just graduating from college. It shows that you are serious, take initiative, and have worked in a professional setting before.

What advice do you have for college students preparing look for their first job in an industry?

They should start networking within companies they think they want to work for. Last fall, I received an e-mail from a student who was going to graduate in the spring. He just wanted to talk for ten minutes and learn about my company, the types of entry-level positions we typically hire for, and ask how I got started in my career. It was such a great idea, showing maturity and focus on learning and preparing for the future. Even if I'm swamped, that is a call I'll be sure to take.

CHAPTER VI

LISTEN TO THOSE WHO WERE JUST IN YOUR SHOES

In this section, I will introduce you to colleagues who have done a fantastic job of transitioning from academic life into professional careers. Each of the following contributors was asked to answer the same two questions from the section above:

- *What did you do in college to prepare yourself for landing your first job in your area of study?*

- *What advice do you have for college students preparing to look for their first job in an industry?*

Chase Kreuter
Account Executive, Conductor, Inc.

Chase Kreuter is one of the most talented young professionals I've ever gotten to know. I met Chase while she was a summer intern at MRM//McCann in New York City. When her internship ended, I knew that I wanted to have her on my team once she was finished with school. Lo and behold, it happened. I had the pleasure of working directly with Chase for three and a half years.

I remember staring at rolling hills of cornfields and cow pastures while my mom and I listened to CDs that I'd burned specifically for the college tour road trip. We discussed what I was looking for in a college—factors like size, courses, sports, community, location. All of these seemed to be important until I pulled up to the hill atop Kenyon College's campus. Immediately, I forgot how many people Kenyon had or how far I was from home. Instead, I felt it instantly. A connection to a place, a comfort in the people, and a sense of community. I was home.

Everyone chooses a college for different reasons— some are looking to the future and thinking about the next step after college. Some wonder how well this school will prepare them for their careers, while others select majors based on careers that interest them. I was not one of these people; I made my decision on a gut instinct and a feeling about the community. The commonality here is the pursuit of a path that aligns to your personality and passions.

During my time at Kenyon College, that same inner voice that drove me to attend the school also drove my selection of activities and courses. I loved how Kenyon allowed me to build a curriculum that fit my interests exactly. I majored in American Studies, an interdisciplinary major that allowed me to take courses across the fields of history, sociology, literature, and art history to uncover my own perspective on the Americans in Paris in the 1920s and their collective experience as the Lost Generation. I got to read, write, travel, and even create my own mock museum. I loved every minute, even the late nights in the library I spent questioning the impact and meaning of the work I was doing. How many times have we all asked—what is the point of all this?

Along the way, my parents would remind me of the importance of maximizing my summers. Work ethic has been a core value of our family, and it would be unacceptable for me to return home every summer without a job lined up. How could I possibly find a job? I didn't know what I was interested in. The only things that aligned to my field of study were art, museums, history—but I am way too loud to work in a museum, and I break things all the time. The saying "bull in a China shop" applies to me. So I started talking to people, anyone and everyone, who had insight on real-world career options.

My dad was a huge resource for this. He would remind me of the amazing careers our family friends had built and that there were plenty of people around me to speak with who might broaden my perspective on what I wanted to do. I had to change my perception of people; Mr. Dowley was no longer the dad in the family I babysat for, but Mr. Dowley the Ad Exec that had led marketing initiatives for some of the biggest brands out there. I was a bit afraid because I thought I would sound stupid. I didn't even know the right questions to ask! I remember the feeling in my stomach when I picked up the phone to call family friends to ask about their careers and scope potential internship opportunities. I felt like I was going to be sick . . . every single time.

The summer after my sophomore year at Kenyon, I landed my first internship in New York City at McCann Erickson. This was not something my college helped me find or something that aligned to my field of study. Instead, it was the result of a relationship I had developed as a babysitter in high school.

I was one of ten summer interns. All of the rest had degrees in Marketing or Advertising . . . I knew nothing. I developed some amazing skills: competitive analysis, market research, project management, humility. I was far from my comfort zone for the majority of the summer. The one comfort I did find was in the people at McCann and the agency community. I connected with the Account Team I worked with and the HR team who led the internship program. When the summer wrapped up, I gave everyone on my team a bottle of wine to thank them for taking me under their wings and trusting me with real client work.

I was grateful for a new understanding of the professional world and what my future might look like. I now knew about industry publications like *AdAge* and *AdWeek*, so I kept up on current events. This helped me establish a bit of a voice and perspective on advertising. Aside from building my confidence, I learned a few things about myself: I learn very quickly, and my natural desire to build relationships is something that I can make a career of.

These lessons drove me to maintain these relationships I had developed and trust in my new knowledge. I knew I wanted my next internship to be in digital, so when I picked up the phone and sent out e-mail outreach about an internship, the stomach dropped a little less. I revisited the connections I had made and called upon family friends in marketing to learn more about how to move into digital. In an e-mail exchange with Mark Dowley, that family friend who soon became a mentor of mine, I learned about a book called *The Search* by John Battelle. I read every page, and it drove my interest and excitement about digital even further.

I found myself back in New York for an interview for a summer internship at MRM//McCann, the sister agency of McCann Erickson that is focused on digital and performance marketing. I was interviewing for an Account Management internship role and

spoke passionately about the book that had been recommended to me—it was all about how Google had
changed the face of marketing forever. As I spoke to
the recruiter, he saw another role for me, one on the
Search Team. So he brought me down to Jorie Water-
man's office. She showed me pivot tables of consum-
er's keyword data and how she had created these awe-
some reports to show her clients how they were getting
found through the organic search channel. While I
told her I knew nothing about Search outside of the
book I read, she took a chance on me.

The summer I worked with Jorie and the MRM//
McCann Search Team, I learned the foundational elements of getting found by search engines and what
that means for a business. I felt like I was starting to
piece together my internship experiences, guidance
from mentors, the industry readings, and even my liberal arts degree. I was analyzing keywords and con-
sumer search behavior the same way I would dissect
a Hemingway novel or a Picasso painting—finding
meaning and perspective in every word. This internship taught me that I loved the linguistic and business
aspect of Search. I can see the importance of the channel as a driver of business insights. I could see myself
exploring this further—so I did. I wrapped up that

summer internship with a presentation of a deliverable I had been working on that outlined all of the strategic insights and findings I had uncovered from analyzing all the ways consumers search for the US Army.

Outside of the professional lessons I took with me, I experienced a community and a work environment that I felt I was a part of. The team inspired me, mentored me, and put a smile on my face every day. When looking to the future, I could not imagine not having those qualities in a work place.

During my senior year, I did not focus on finding the perfect job, like many others in my class. Instead, my focus was on my work, my activities, my friends, and taking in every minute of my last year on Kenyon's campus. I did, however, maintain and nurture the relationships I made over the summer. I visited with the team for lunch when I was back on breaks from school and exchanged e-mails whenever possible. During this time, I came to understand what my professional experience post-college needed to include: strong leadership, constant learning, passionate community, and opportunity for growth. Understanding this helped me to navigate landing a job because I knew what I was looking for. The industry may have varied in the conversations I was having and the roles

I was speaking about, but good company values and culture were things I knew for certain that I needed.

I didn't get every job I interviewed for. But when the MRM//McCann Search Team was ready to hire, I got the call to interview, and I got the job. I never could have imagined my first job out of college being in Organic Search, and I hadn't even known this marketing channel existed until the year prior. But I knew this was a place where I could learn a lot and launch into an area of business that fascinated me.

My experience in navigating my career, from internships, my first job, and beyond, has taught me lessons that I share with any recent graduate who calls looking for guidance. Here is my advice:

Cultivate your network and learn about your friends and family members in their professional context. Don't know where to start? Ask about a book they love about the industry they work in. Read it, ask questions, and engage.

Don't worry about what or whom you want to be for the rest of your life. Explore different industries. Your career choice won't define you. You will be bringing your passions and the person you are to the company you choose.

Know what atmosphere you thrive in and find a

company and community that will help you grow both professionally and personally. You will likely spend more time with your coworkers than your family. When you speak with companies, ask questions about their company values and leadership. This is just as much your opportunity to learn about them as it is theirs to learn about you.

Be humble and honest. Don't be afraid to ask questions and admit you don't know answers to certain questions. On the other side of that, be confident in what you do know. Most importantly, be confident in yourself.

Lastly, as my mom would say, always send a thank-you note. An e-mail after a phone conversation or in-person meeting thanking someone for their time is key to nurturing that relationship. If you are excited by an opportunity or inspired by someone enough, send a handwritten one too. While this is business, we are all human and mustn't lose sight of how creating personal connections with others can guide our paths forward.

Laurel Marcus

Sr. Manager, SEO & Digital Experience at Tank Design

I met Laurel when I managed the search and content strategy team at MRM//McCann in New York City. Laurel was part of a working rotational program that allowed new college graduates to experience different areas of an agency before deciding where they wanted to focus. Our team was in the middle of a labor-intensive project that needed help. I reached out to a colleague in a different department and asked if he had any spare hands I could borrow for a few days. He offered up Laurel.

From day one, Laurel was a rock star. Her quality of work, speed, and commitment to the project were second to none. Laurel asked really good questions and challenged well-thought-out assumptions. Laurel is the type of person every manager wants on their team—and I somehow managed to convince her to join mine.

Laurel continues to excel in her career as the Senior Manager of SEO & Digital Experience at Tank Design in Cambridge, Massachusetts. I consider Laurel to be a close friend, a sister, and someone I'd love the opportunity to work with again.

What did you do in college to prepare yourself for landing your first job in your area of study?

Knowing that my resume was my first chance to make a strong impression with potential employers, I understood that this simple one-pager represented a lot more than just what I'd been up to for the past four years. Especially because I studied something slightly off the beaten path with a major in Middle Eastern Studies and a minor in Digital Arts, and I was seeking job opportunities in an entirely different industry, I knew my resume had to work hard for me. My college facilitated a career program where undergraduate seniors were paired with students in the business school to workshop their resumes. I learned that what I considered to be my most significant or time-consuming activity wasn't necessarily the most impactful activity to highlight. Discussing my undergraduate experience with this business student teased out the activities that would drive relevance and intrigue with employers and ultimately help me get my foot in the door.

What should college students a year or two away from graduation start doing now to prepare for landing their first job?

1. Become an exceptional writer. Because it's incredibly hard to see past a poorly written cover letter or resume. And because nothing will replace the human ability to communicate, no matter how much technology evolves, honing this craft will make you more articulate and will make your message more compelling. No matter what industry you land in, your ability to compel others and communicate will be invaluable.

2. Go on as many interviews as possible, even if you're only moderately interested in a position. Use each interview to practice how to reframe your sound bites, to learn what employers are interested learning, and to identify what topics you don't have a sound bite prepared for. If you're equipped to answer anything, this will help you feel confident and will make you appear confident too (no matter how fast your heart is beating or how sweaty your palms are).

Amanda Irel Sajecki

Manager, Insights & Planning, VaynerMedia

Amanda was a new admin at MRM//McCann and was incredibly warm when we met the first time. I immediately knew that she and I would be good friends. Over the course of the next few months and years, Amanda and I had long conversations about our industry and her career path. We also spent a significant amount of time talking about the WWE, which is a brand we both love and engage with on a regular basis.

Amanda had big dreams that stretched much further than her administrative position, and I watched Amanda turn her dreams into reality. In a few short years, Amanda received multiple promotions and got the role she wanted at MRM. She later landed a social media strategy job at the WWE. To say I was jealous would be an understatement.

Amanda's life and career has been one of over-coming adversity and winning. As I started putting the outline together for *Hopeful to Hired*, I knew that Amanda's perspective needed to be included.

What did you do in college to prepare yourself for landing your first job in your area of study?

As an indecisive college student who couldn't figure out what I wanted to do in life, I did little of the typical job preparation recommended to college students. I didn't have internships, real world experiences, or a job offer upon graduation. It was 2009 and the recession had just eliminated the job market.

But needing money and wanting responsibility, I hustled to find opportunities—and made the most of every opportunity provided to me. For the first few years out of college, I took jobs beneath my skill level and sometimes with family at local businesses, even as my mother's assistant, to build up my resume. Even though working for my mother was frustrating, I took on as much work as possible to prove my skills and learn more about her world of small business advertising. Eventually I worked my way up from my mother's assistant to the manager of digital marketing and social media at the company.

When I yearned to move beyond the small business world and get into the corporate world of advertising, I swallowed my pride and took an entry-level assistant job at an agency just to get my foot in the door. I spent months booking travel and buying lunches for executives, but I also immediately offered to help in doing any extra work I could get my hands on.

Whether the strategy team needed research, the executive team needed social content ideas, or the new business team needed shopper insights, I offered to stay late, come in on weekends, and travel to help out in any way I could. When the analytics team was evaluating their resource portfolio, I jumped to offer to research analytics tools and vendors, teaching myself about data analysis and the industry's top measurement tools to offer a smart analysis of the most useful vendors for my boss's department.

Oftentimes I wasn't met with the most confidence, being the lowly assistant, but I grew a thick skin and for a year and a half begged for opportunities to do "real work."

I was lucky to be surrounded by people who admired my persistence, and after three years of hustling through assistant jobs, my willingness to do research and attention to detail paid off. I was officially given a "real" position working in strategy.

What should college students a year or two away from graduation start doing now to prepare for landing their first job?

While several internships are expected from today's graduates, there is more that college students can do to differentiate themselves from the pack. It's not always about the traditional, recognizable job to jumpstart your career. Sometimes it's necessary to make the most of the opportunities available or hustle to create your own.

Share your knowledge. Start a blog where you can display your skills—whether it's strategy, sociology, graphic design, or fashion, create a website where you can proactively create content. Though your blog may not have tons of readers, it can help show evidence for the skills that your resume says you possess.

Lend your skills. Reach out to local businesses or friends who might benefit from your services. If you want a career in social media content, offer to be a community manager for a local salon or bakery. If you're a photographer looking for a paid gig, offer to shoot some shows for a local music venue or portraits for a school.

Collaborate with professors. Your college professors can be your greatest assets when you're looking to gain work experience. They likely know of local professionals looking for assistance. Helping local professionals on a project or specific occasion can end up not only as a resume item, but also as a networking opportunity. Some professors might also need help in their "day jobs," whether it's research, data entry, or simple creative work. And finally, some professors may even give you the opportunity to collaborate on creating their next teaching topics or even course curriculum. Having the ability to think "big picture" about your field of interest to help a professor create course materials can also be a great way to build up a resume in your college years.

My path proves that if you remain humble and eager, you can achieve anything despite your college circumstances. Don't wait to find open doors; open them yourself!

Samantha Steinbring
Online Affiliate Marketing Specialist at Deluxe Corporation

A few years ago, I led a session at the Student Ad Summit event held at the University of Minnesota. During the Q&A section, Sam asked a few good questions and won a prize for her participation. After the presentation, Sam approached me, and we had a fantastic conversation.

Sam and I met a few weeks later for an informational interview over breakfast that turned into a great friendship. With her intelligence, desire to learn, and dedication, I knew Sam would be a valuable asset to any company that hired her. So when a position opened up on my team at Deluxe, I made her an offer.

I worked with Sam side-by-side for three years before she transitioned into a different role within our department. I've watched Sam grow from a brilliant college student into a world-class professional. I'm honored that Sam believed so much in *Hopeful to Hired* that she wanted to contribute. Sam has a big heart for college students and regularly pays it forward.

Sam attributes much of her career success to her mom for instilling in her the virtues of confidence, passion, and hard work.

What did you do in college to prepare yourself for landing your first job in your area of study?

When I was going to college, it was very important to me to take advantage of every resource available to set myself up for success when it came time to searching for my first job. As a sophomore I learned all about the importance of networking, and to put that into practice, I started developing professional relationships with adjunct professors in my program. The adjunct professors had many years of experience in advertising, my field of study, and they were always willing to help students make real world connections to professionals in the industry. I reached out via e-mail to people in my professors' networks and started doing informational interviews to learn more about different companies and different roles I could pursue. In addition to informational interviews, I attended various networking events and career fairs hosted by my university. One of the most important events I attended, the Student Advertising Summit, taught me so much about the industry I was pursuing. I saw an opportunity to make more connections and develop additional skills, so I joined the planning committee for the event. I started as a junior committee member and eventually became director of the event. This experience allowed me to make many more connections in the industry, and it eventually led to me landing my first job.

What should college students a year or two from graduation start doing now to prepare for landing their first job?

Every college student preparing to land their first job should start doing three things right now: network within their industry, build their professional portfolio, and develop skills and experience. Showing initiative and being proactive by e-mailing professionals in the field, asking questions, setting up informational interviews, and following up on those meetings will set you far apart from other students. Then, when it's time to start job hunting, you can reach out to the networking connections you've made and ask about open positions. The key with networking, however, is to be genuine and to form mutually beneficial relationships. Try to bring something to the table—a unique point of view, knowledge of industry trends, specific questions that show you've done your research, etc.—so that you can cultivate a truly professional relationship, rather than a relationship solely based on your needs.

As you begin networking and developing relationships in the industry, you also need to set yourself apart on paper. Your resume, in many cases, is what will land you an interview. Make sure your resume reflects your experience and your professionalism. Use your college's career resources to have your resume reviewed. Ask your professors, friends, and family members to review it as well. In addition to your resume, it is important to portray yourself professionally online. Many students create online resumes and portfolios, which can give them an edge when job searching. Your public social media profiles should reflect your career ambitions and professional demeanor as well because prospective employers will view them.

Finally, try to get experience in your field. Target positions in your major's administration office, or seek out volunteer opportunities and organizations that will help you gain practical experience in your area of study. Taking on these types of roles will give you real world experience while you are still in school, which you can talk about on your resume and in interviews. Employers like to see that you are invested in your field of study beyond the classroom, so taking leadership roles in clubs and organizations can greatly improve your chances of landing a great first job out of college.

Alex Masica
New Media Manager, Minnesota Lottery

I asked Alex to contribute to *Hopeful to Hired* because he's amassed a wide variety of professional experience in a short amount of time. In other words, he's a go-getter. Alex appreciates working on smaller teams as it allows him to learn new skills that he might not have learned working in a larger group. Alex is an incredibly creative person who has found much success post graduation.

What did you do in college to prepare yourself for landing your first job in your area of study?
I had many honest conversations with professors and community mentors about what I wanted to do and what employers would be looking for in someone straight out of college. Based on their advice, I made

sure I did a few key things really well in order to stand out from my competition:

Create a professional online presence: I had a decent portfolio of graphic design and public relations work that needed an online home. I set up a website and a blog to highlight it and showed my process for getting from an idea to a finished product. Additionally, I made sure my LinkedIn profile was complete and up to date, including a couple of recommendations. I also spent my last couple of years in college building my network through Twitter and crafting my online brand. All of these things together created a really cohesive online presence for me where it was easy to understand who I was as a person—both personally and professionally—and what I was looking to do in my career.

Over-prepare for the interview process: Looking back, one of the best ways my professors set me up for success was giving great critical feedback on things like my resume, answers I had prepared for common interview questions, what I should wear to different types of interviews, and questions to ask employers. Some of these might seem like common sense, but my professors challenged my thinking and point of view, which in the end helped me craft a stronger story for myself and also helped me to walk in looking and acting as professional as possible.

Network with as many people as you can—I went to school in a mid-sized city in a time when LinkedIn was just becoming popular. During my junior and senior years of college, I connected with as many people in the community as I could to get my name out there and let them know who I was, what I had to offer, what I wanted to do, and also to offer my help in any way I could. I did the same thing with many of my peers and classmates. By getting in front of a sizeable amount of people, I became the person that hiring managers thought of when an internship or entry-level job opened up at their respective companies or when someone asked them for a referral.

What should college students, a year or two away from graduation, start doing now to prepare for landing their first job?

My biggest piece of advice is to create and refine your personal brand, and find ways to get it in front of prospective employers in new and unique ways. Breaking it down, here is what I recommend you focus on:

Take as many internships as you can: Do whatever you can to get your feet wet in the industry you want to enter after college. Consider taking an internship outside of your industry, too. Even though I did not want to work in the nonprofit world, the internship I took at a community resource center changed the way I look at assistance programs and also taught me how to get creative with marketing strategies and tactics since there was not any money in the budget to do fancy campaigns. By taking as many internships as you can, you not only gain valuable experience and widen your lens on doing great work, but you also have great content with which to fill your resume.

Make sure employers find you online: It should not be a surprise that nearly every employer will Google your name at some point before hiring you. Use this to your advantage by winning the search results for your name with things like a Twitter profile, a LinkedIn account, a website, or a blog. By doing this, you own the narrative about your brand. It also shows that you know how to create and maintain content online. Depending on what kind of job you hope to find, understanding content strategy can help get your resume to the top of the pile.

Network, network, network: Networking, by nature, is not the most enjoyable experience. Some people love it, but most people hate it. But it is still necessary and extremely beneficial. Attend job fairs, cocktail mixers, informational presentations, or ask people directly out for a drink or coffee. By meeting people in the industry you want to enter, you are expanding your network and letting people know you exist. Most positions are filled by an internal or direct referral. If you are going to get in the door, you have to know someone on the inside.

Perfect the heck out of your resume: If you do nothing else, make sure your resume is as perfect as possible. Have professors, mentors, peers, family, and friends read through your resume, and welcome their feedback. Does your wording make sense? Is it free of grammatical errors? Does the most important content catch people's attention? Is it correctly formatted or designed for your respective industry? Your resume is your first impression for employers—make sure it is perfect. I cannot stress enough how important it is to pay attention to the fine details of your resume. A simple punctuation or grammatical error could mean the difference between you and the next resume in the stack getting a call for an interview.

A FINAL
ENCOURAGEMENT

What you've just finished reading is both a philosophical and tactical approach to preparing yourself while you're in college for success after graduation. While the book is fairly straightforward, it requires a time investment and steady commitment to fully see the benefits.

I am well aware that taking on the career preparation that this book recommends in addition to your current classwork may be intimidating. But I promise that it's worth the sacrifice. As you begin to grow your professional network, improve your soft skills, and create an online presence that best represents your personal brand, you'll find that your confidence will grow.

What I want you to know is that whether you're a freshman entering college or a college senior, you can do this! If you're a freshman, you have a longer timeframe to work on the advice that this book gives. If you're further in your college career, you may have a shorter runway. Either way, I recommend putting a plan together to help you avoid burnout and discouragement. Here are a few practical ideas to consider:

Make Small and Tangible Goals: Some of you may be working a full-time job, like I did, to pay your way through college. You may have a family to take care of while attending college. You may be a single parent who already feels overwhelmed with your responsibilities. The key here is not to bite off more than you can chew. You, more than anyone, know your limits. Push hard, stretch yourself, but most important—take care of yourself. Put a plan together that makes sense for you. Set small and tangible goals, and work toward them.

Reward Yourself: As you accomplish the goals that you've set for yourself, make sure to celebrate the wins. Maybe the first goal you've set in preparing to find your first job after graduation is to read this book. In that case, when you're finished reading, have a night out with your friends. It may sound silly, but recognizing our own accomplishments, as small as we think they are, can provide the much-needed fuel to keep us going.

Find an Accountability Partner: An accountability partner is someone you ask to hold you accountable for achieving goals you've set. They're also responsible for being a source of encouragement. For instance, when I was writing *Hopeful to Hired*, my good friend, Lynn McDaniel, checked in on me on a regular basis. She made sure that I wasn't letting the distractions in life prevent me from finishing. Start thinking about whom you trust to hold you accountable. If you have a friend who is also reading this book, keep each other accountable. There's nothing like having someone who's going through the same process you are to keep you accountable.

Finally, thank you for reading *Hopeful to Hired*. This book is a passion project based on my experience and my heart for college students preparing for post-collegiate success. Feel free to contact me on hopefultohired.com. I will personally respond to as many of you as time allows.

BIBLIOGRAPHY

Adams, Susan. "The Test That Measures A Leader's Strength." *Forbes*, August 28, 2009. http://www.forbes.com/2009/08/28/strengthsfinder-skills-test-leadership-managing-jobs.html.

"Body Language Quiz: Test Your Emotional Intelligence." *Greater Good: The Science of a Meaningful Life*. http://greatergood.berkeley.edu/ei_quiz/.

Boushey, Heather, and Sarah Jane Glynn. "There Are Significant Business Costs to Replacing Employees." *Center for American Progress*, November 16, 2012. https://www.americanprogress.org/wp-content/uploads/2012/11/CostofTurnover.pdf.

Goleman, Daniel. "What Makes a Leader?" *Harvard Business Review*, January, 2004. https://hbr.org/2004/01/what-makes-a-leader.

Golis, Chris. "A Brief History of Emotional Intelligence." *Practical Emotional Intelligence.* http://www.emotionalintelligencecourse.com/eq-history.

Hadzima, Joe. "How Much Does an Employee Cost?" *Boston Business Journal.* http://web.mit.edu/e-club/hadzima/pdf/how-much-does-an-employee-cost.pdf.

Han, Lei. "Soft Skill Definition: What Are Soft Skills?" *Soft Skills—Ask a Wharton MBA.* https://bemycareercoach.com/softskills/what-are-soft-skills.

MBTI. Last modified 2016. https://www.mbtionline.com/.

Miller, Nicole. "A Step-by-Step Guide To Hosting or Joining a Twitter Chat." *Buffer Blog*, August 20, 2014. https://blog.bufferapp.com/twitter-chat-101.